Healing Manic Depression and Depression

WHAT WORKS
Based On What Helped Me

Mary Beth Smith

First Print Edition: August 2013

Dedicated to Linda Cross, M.D.
The psychiatrist who helped me most.

One does not become fully human painlessly.—Rollo May

In 1984, the author had a psychotic mania which nearly caused her to lose her life. Afterwards she plunged into a severe depression which was even more horrible. She resolved to seek help. She was raped by her first psychiatrist so she switched to a new one who was most helpful. Over the years she made steady progress in her quest for mental health. This book explains the methods that helped her achieve her goal.

Healing Manic Depression and Depression, What Works contains descriptions of the bipolar disorders and facts your doctor doesn't have time to tell you. It explains, for example, why you may feel a definite cognitive loss that feels like a brain injury; why you gain weight on your medications; why bipolar disorder runs in over-achieving families; how dangerous postpartum psychosis is; and why some of us are so creative. Next, it tells the author's story which differs a little from others in that she didn't become ill until reaching middle-age, when her life and career were fairly well established. It shows how her father influenced her with his example of courage in the face of polio. It also shows many of the difficulties bipolar and depressed people face, such as stigma, loss of the ability to do their current job, personal mistakes made as a result of loneliness, trouble with psychiatrists and the lack of good psychotherapy which forces them to read these self-help books in the first place! There is a chapter on how to confront paranoia and other neuroses and look at situations in a different light. Since Alcoholics Anonymous (A.A.) has helped so many alcoholics become mentally healthy, the book examines how A.A. does this. And it explains what mental health really is, what self-actualization is and offers suggestions of historical figures to read about and imitate. It is short, but readable. Also it is well-researched.

Table of Contents

Healing Manic Depression and Depression

Introduction

The more literally lost you are, the more literally you are the very being whom Christ's sacrifice has already saved.—Martin Luther

In 1900 Clifford Beers, a college graduate from a middle class family, dropped from a four story window breaking both his feet and severely injuring his back. His suicide attempt resulted in much time spent in mental institutions which were horrible at the time.

On March 27, 1932 Hubert, a friend of my father's, was happily shuffling several duties at once: waiting tables, attending the University of Chicago, dating and attending swim practice. He often waited on prominent men ("You may have heard of Thornton Wilder"). He was already looking for a summer job. Three weeks later he called my father asking how my great uncle Elmer killed himself. My father in his rather clear and simple way, described the method.

The next day Hubert killed himself in the same fashion. My father, of course, felt terrible.

In 1977, my father, a self-actualized man if I ever saw one, became manic after being given a tricyclic antidepressant. My normally frugal, quiet, well behaved father became loud and raucous: foolishly spending money; insisting on getting in touch with people he hadn't seen in forty years; flying to San Francisco, a 3000 mile one day trip (to see the bridges). My mother took his antidepressants away and he plunged into a deep depression which lasted until 1982, when he died. In October of 1984, after unbearable pressure at work and home, I became manic. Believing I would be reincarnated, I pointed my Volkswagen Beetle towards a tree and sped up to 75 mph. I hit the tree which resulted in a collapsed lung, broken ribs, a broken ankle and the loss of a considerable amount of blood.

Bipolar disorder is thought to be genetic. Certainly we who have it know it is not our fault. The only good thing it does is make us aware of the fact that we are weak and need help. This book suggests relying on your *higher power* which I will explain later. If you do the things suggested by this book you will get better. Suicidal thoughts will go away. Paranoia will become easy to handle. You will be able to *talk yourself* out of depression. Medication may still be necessary but I have read that people who have major depression may be able, with the help of their doctors, to eliminate those medications entirely.

I used cognitive therapy to help treat my obsessive thoughts. Cognitive therapy is now known to partially correct your condition by changing the structure of your brain. But since the psychic pain is so great, we also need something faster acting. This is what the medication is for. You may have to take those pills for perhaps years, or the rest of your life especially if you have one of the bipolar disorders. Recurrent depression is thought to be related to bipolar disorder. As such, you may need to keep taking antidepressants. Self-help books are a huge help also. They are thought to be as helpful in healing the brain as cognitive therapy itself.

I am better now because of practicing the suggestions in this book. Work with your doctor. Don't change your medications on your own. It is a recipe for disaster. I do notice that people who have used these suggestions are much calmer than those who don't. These are methods worth trying. Good luck in your search for mental health.

1

Manic-Depressive Illnesses and Recurrent Depression

My mind was beginning to have to scramble a bit to keep up with itself, as ideas were coming so fast that they intersected one another at every conceivable angle. There was a neuronal pileup on the highways of my brain, and the more I tried to slow down my thinking the more I became aware that I couldn't. My enthusiasms were going into overdrive as well, although there often was some underlying thread of logic in what I was doing.—Kay Redfield Jamison, *An Unquiet Mind*

Mania

Common signs of mania and hypomania are as follows:

- elevated mood
- decreased need for sleep
- rapid speech
- fast thinking
- inflated self-esteem
- poor judgement
- risk taking
- spending too much money [1]

Unlike mania, hypomania doesn't affect your ability to function. It can cause excessive involvement in pleasurable but dangerous activities. If followed by depression the depression can be severe and frequent. The mild form of hypomania is quite productive. [2] Unlike hypomania, mania does affect your ability to function and sometimes includes bizarre behavior, grandiose delusions, and/or visual and auditory hallucinations. [3] It can also include elation.

Theodore Roethke said, "I didn't sleep much. I just walked around with this wonderful feeling." Robert Lowell said, "I believed I could stop cars and paralyze their forces by merely standing in the middle of the highway with my arms outspread...." [4]

The aftermath of mania is usually depression. Before lithium, fully 1/5 of manic-depressives died by suicide. Today 1/4 to 1/2 of patients have attempted suicide at least once. [5]

Depression

The most common symptom of depression is "diminished interest or pleasure in all or almost all activities."

Other signs are:

- changes in appetite
- changes in sleep patterns
- loss of motivation
- feelings of guilt
- inability to concentrate
- slowing of speech, thought and movement
- recurring thoughts of death or suicide [6]

French composer Hector Berlioz wrote, "One's only wish is for silence, solitude and the oblivion of sleep...nothing has meaning...."

Austrian composer Hugo Wolf wrote, "I would like most to hang myself on the nearest branch of the cherry trees standing now in full bloom." [7] F. Scott Fitzgerald wrote, "Every act of life from the morning toothbrush to the friend at dinner had become an effort…." Poet Edward Thomas wrote, "I am weary of everything. I stay because I am too weak to go." [8]

Bipolar I, bipolar II and recurrent depression are included by some scientists in manic-depressive illness. Recurrent means that the major depression occurred more than once. Abraham Lincoln had at least 2 major depressions. One when he was found lying on the grave of his first love in the rain and the other when he broke up with his fiance Mary Todd. His friends had to hide all sharp objects from him after the break-up.

Cyclothymia

Cyclothymia is the mildest form of manic-depressive illness. It consists of alternating moods of hypomania and depression. [9] It usually starts in adolescence or early adulthood. The patient may go on to develop bipolar I. [10]

Bipolar I

Bipolar I is the most severe form of the illness. An episode can begin with hyperactivity. The person usually then becomes agitated, paranoid and shows signs of grandiosity. 50 percent become unable to distinguish reality from fantasy. [11]

Bipolar II

Bipolar II is hypomania alternating with periods of depression. Many people go undiagnosed because they only seek help for the depression. [12] It impairs the person's functioning at work and at home. It is not considered bipolar II if the symptoms are brought on by an antidepressant or other medications. [13]

Bipolar NOS

Bipolar NOS (not otherwise specified) does not meet any other criteria. It may not last long enough; it may be a hypomanic episode without depressive symptoms; it may be caused by a medication or underlying health condition; it may be superimposed on another disorder. [14]

Mixed Mania

Mixed mania is where "both mania and depression occur simultaneously, or alternate frequently during the day." [15]

Postpartum Depression and Psychosis

Only 1 in 1,000 women get postpartum psychosis or depression. Without treatment it lasts for months. It is thought to be related to manic-depressive illness because the symptoms are almost identical.

Bipolar women are at high risk of getting it (50-75 percent). They are treated with lithium before the birth and lithium or other mood stabilizers afterwards. Since sleep disruptions cause mania, they should not be allowed to care for their infant during the first 6 weeks after birth. [16]

25 percent of bipolar women had their bipolar disorder triggered by postpartum psychosis. [17] Woman who have already had postpartum problems have a 50 percent chance of having it again at future births. While the woman is in the later stages of pregnancy, lithium is given because it is much less likely to harm the fetus than the other mood stabilizers valproate and carbamazepine.

Andrea Yates was known to have problems with postpartum psychosis. Her husband was told to never leave her alone. He left her alone for 1 hour and she methodically drowned each of her 5 children. She called 911 and said, "I just killed my kids."

In her first trial she was found guilty. The verdict was overturned on appeal, and in her second trial she was declared not guilty by reason of insanity. She now has been diagnosed with bipolar disorder and lives in a State Hospital where she is given some freedom. Her lawyer hopes she will be freed soon. He is now dedicated to educating the public about women's mental health problems.

Shelley Ash had never heard of postpartum psychosis when she became pregnant. She got it "out of the blue." When she found herself with an urge to kill the baby, she ran to the bathroom and took an overdose of pain killers. She survived and has since devoted her time to spreading information about the illness. [18]

After having a baby, Melanie Stokes was so depressed that she could no longer eat, drink or swallow. She started to dream up ways of killing herself. She was put in the hospital several times. One time after she got out of the hospital she jumped out of a 12 story window, killing herself. Her parents are now trying to inform the public about this illness. [19]

Stress

Manic-depressive illness is first triggered by some major life stress. Life events that trigger the illness include losing a loved one, changing jobs, and moving. It only happens if the person has inherited a genetic vulnerability to the illness. Just over 1 percent of people have some form of the illness. 1 person in 20 will have a major depression over their lifetime. [20] Patients find subsequent episodes harder to explain. [21]

If manic-depression and recurrent depression are not treated properly they will occur more often and worsen over time. [22]

Genetics

Bipolar disorder and recurrent depression run in families due to a genetic vulnerability. [23] It may require 3 or more such genes to produce a vulnerability. [24] The individual carrying the genes may never get the illness but they may pass it on to their children. [25] If an identical twin has bipolar disorder the likelihood of the other twin having it is 70 to 100 percent. In fraternal twins it is 20 percent. If one parent has manic-depression the likelihood of their child getting it is 28 percent. If one parent is bipolar and the other has a mood disorder the likelihood is 75 percent. [26]

Creativity

Healthy writers are more productive when they are hypomanic. Bipolar or unipolar writers do better when they are in a normal mood. [27]

People with mood disorders are gifted in many ways and their siblings are more likely to be gifted also. IQ does not seem to relate very much to creativity. The great creative genius in physics, Richard Feynman, only had an IQ in the low 120's. [28]

A disproportionate number of great writers and artists have suffered from "bipolar spectrum disorders" and "under some circumstances, creativity can be facilitated by such disorders." [29]

One study examined eminent poets, writers and artists. The poets were 50 percent more likely than the general public to have been treated for a mood disorder. Biographers were the least likely to suffer from such disorders.

The list below shows some poets and their symptoms.

- Samuel Johnson - severe recurrent melancholia
- William Blake - hallucinations
- Robert Burns - severe recurrent melancholia
- William Wordsworth - moody and violent temper
- Sir Walter Scott - melancholy
- Samuel Taylor Coleridge - despair, grandiose and agitated
- Robert Southey - unduly excitable
- George Gordon, Lord Byron - recurrent melancholia, rage
- John Clare - 25 years in an insane asylum, hallucinations
- John Keats - periods of depression followed by periods of intense activity and exhilaration [30]

IQ

People with bipolar disorder are born with an above average IQ. But the disorder is currently believed to cause a deterioration in IQ when the disease first expresses itself. This deterioration appears to be permanent.

The IQ test is made up of 2 parts—verbal (VIQ) and non-verbal (PIQ). Studies show that the verbal part remains high but the nonverbal part becomes lower than average. The PIQ tests most influenced by bipolar disorder include picture arrangement, picture completion, object assembly, and block design. [31] "This differential deficit is relatively constant across states of euthymia [normal mood], depression, and mania...." [32]

Middle and Upper Classes

Bipolar illness is over represented in the professional and upper classes. The families have become successful perhaps because of their high IQ's and because of the achievements of some of the hypomanic family members. Hypomanic people are likable, energetic, creative, funny and self-confident. They are also noticeably moody but people put up with their moods because they are so popular. They do well in their chosen field. [33]

Weight Gain

Atypical antipsychotics in the short term can cause a minor weight gain. With some of the atypical antipsychotics the weight gain doesn't level off. It causes an increase in appetite and people continue to gain weight for several months. The weight gain is of the abdominal type—the most dangerous. That type causes insulin resistance and cardiovascular problems. [34]

Lithium can cause a 5 to 10 percent weight gain. People sometimes stop taking it because of that. It has an effect on carbohydrate metabolism including a mild anti-insulin effect. A doctor recently told me to restrict carbohydrates and continue going to my Weight Watchers meetings. After a psychotic episode I had become obese and my ankles were swollen. After more than 2 years I lost about 40 pounds by religiously going to the meetings and dieting. Psychiatrists now recommend regular exercise, restriction of sugary drinks, avoidance of simple carbohydrates, taking atypical antipsychotics that do not cause weight gain, avoiding some antidepressants and avoiding some conventional antipsychotics. [35]

Medication

There is no cure for bipolar disorder. Bipolar disorder is a life-long mental health disorder that can be treated well with certain medications, but it will never go away. Fortunately there are a lot of good drugs out there to treat bipolar, and if your relative works with a psychiatrist who can help them find the right dose of the right drug they can lead a relatively normal life with few interruptions from their disease. [36]

Doctors now agree that it is malpractice to treat depressive and manic-depressive illness without medication. [37]

The medication *does* work and is recommended by nearly every doctor. Jean Marion explained the results well in her blog:

The adultery stopped. The cyber sex, the phone sex, the stealing, the lying, the cheating, the suicidal ideation, the homicidal ideation, it all came to a screeching halt.

She "finally realized that [she] didn't have the power to stop doing stupid and wrong things on [her] own."

Mania and hypomania are treated with mood stabilizers. These can cause tremor, weight gain, cognitive dulling and bad memory. [38]

Untreated, episodes become more frequent and more severe. [39]

Depression is treated with anti-depressants and it is important to continue the medication to prevent recurring depression.

The side effects of anti-depressants may be drowsiness, sedation, headaches and tension. If the side effects become too difficult to handle, the patient can be switched to another medication. Interestingly, lithium maintenance has been shown to lower the risk of suicide.

2

My Story

Life is difficult—M. Scott Peck, *The Road Less Travelled*

When I was born, my parents barely made it to the hospital on time. When my mother got to Mercy hospital she yelled, "I"m having this baby now!" The doctor stopped the contractions by using a *saddle block.*

My mother was narcissistic but very loving as long as I acted like her version of a nice, well-behaved child, which I did until I was about 14.

My father lost the use of both his legs 5 years before I was born. (He had polio.) He bore it bravely from the beginning. He found a way to look at it that he could live with. He then set about helping other polio patients who were in the hospital at the same time.

After he got out of the hospital he found a way to get around with crutches and braces. Then he found a way to drive and was able to go back to his job. He was calm, good looking, nice and funny. Whenever something bad happened to him he managed to turn it into a funny story. He was always smiling.

When I was a toddler I noticed that my 2 teenage sisters as well as my mother almost always had their noses in a book. "Being able to read means that you are a big girl," I thought. The thicker the book the better. This is why I read so much today.

When I was about 3, I closely examined my 2 sisters. Anne, the oldest, looked like a model or a beautiful actress. Her hair was perfect, her finger nails were perfect, her toe nails were perfect, her legs were shaved and her face was fine-featured. This required too much maintenance, I thought.

So I looked at the other one, Sue, who would barely drag a comb through her hair and did not care much about her appearance. But she did paint beautiful pictures, wore an artists smock with a considerable amount of bright colored paint on it, and owned her own pony. Now *she* was interesting.

I decided to be something *in-between*. I would always comb my hair and dress neatly. But I would never compete with Sue's artistic abilities or Anne's glamour. When I was 4, my father showed me a model of a Piper Cub. "I used to fly this kind of airplane," he said. I thought that there only existed big planes flown by airline pilots. I made up my mind, then and there, to learn to fly one day like my father. Flying considerably improved my self-esteem when I was a teenager.

My trouble began when I was 2. My sisters and I were riding in the car with my father when we were hit by another car. I flew out of Sue's arms and hit my head on the dashboard. I don't remember all that, but I do remember going to an old lady's house. I sat in the living room and looked around for a television set. No TV set but I did see a big radio from the 1920's just like one we had. That comforted me.

My father, thinking I had hurt my nose, drove me to Mercy hospital. Doctors there examined my nose. It was very scary having 3 big men look up my nose with a light.

From then on, I had a panic attack whenever someone other than my parents was driving.

I remember going to see Billy, the new baby, at age 5. While my sister was driving down Charles Street in Baltimore, I was overcome by fear and a turning-over feeling in my stomach. I threw myself to the floor and clutched my stomach. "What is wrong," my sisters cried. "My stomach hurts," is all I said.

I had frequent panic attacks from then on. It would happen whenever I felt trapped: in a line of children at school; in church surrounded by people; in car pool when someone other than my mother was driving; driving through a tunnel; landing a plane when I was in my 20's.

I finally solved the problem in my 20's by reciting the *Bene Gesserit Litany Against Fear* from <u>Dune</u>, a science fiction novel by Frank Herbert.

The Litany is as follows:

I must not fear.
Fear is the mind-killer.
Fear is the little-death that brings total obliteration.
I will face my fear.
I will permit it to pass over me and through me.
And when it has gone past I will turn the inner eye to see its path.
Where the fear has been there will be nothing…Only I will remain. [1]

I sometimes had to say this litany on final approach to the runway while being closely watched by a flight instructor. I had to stop the panic attack or possibly crash.

Before I attended kindergarten, I didn't have much exposure to other children. My mother would sometimes take me to see 2 little boys who never opened their mouths. And there was one very nice little girl, a toddler 3 years younger than I, who could barely talk.

I was very quiet. I would (and still do) hesitate to talk until it is too late. It is as if I have something to say but my brain puts a road block in front of it. The thought rarely makes it to my mouth.

This made for a very uncomfortable first day of kindergarten. I walked into the classroom and it seemed to me as if most of the children had singled out another child of the same sex and begun to talk—non-stop. I marveled at this but felt bad that I couldn't do it.

The next thing that happened was that the nun (this was a Catholic school) called out our names, one at a time, and we were supposed to raise our hand when we heard our name. "MARY ELIZABETH JONES," she yelled loudly. I was puzzled. I *thought* that was my name but I wasn't sure. No one had ever called me that. Not wanting to make a mistake, I kept my hand down. I got in trouble for that.

One time she asked all the blue-eyed children to stand in one group and the brown-eyed children to stand in another. I didn't know what color my eyes were. (They are a little bit of everything: blue, green and gray with brown flecks.) A couple of children came over to examine my eyes. "They are blue," one said. "They are brown," said another. "They are green," another said. The nun was disturbed. For that entire school year she labeled me as retarded.

At age 6 I took an IQ test which I quickly completed. "You are smart!" the nun exclaimed, probably expecting a much lower score. I was thrilled! Maybe one day I would be as smart as my teenage sisters.

In first grade we were given a choice of about 100 books to read. I'd often sign out a book and struggle over the words at home. "Sound it out," my mother would say. Also without being told, I did my home work as soon as I got home before I went out to play. This was something I instinctively knew was right, like drinking all your chicken soup and leaving the delicious noodles 'till last. (Leave the best for last is the lesson here.)

That was a Catholic private school and the best school I ever went to. When I was in 3rd grade, my father switched us to a Catholic parochial school where I learned almost nothing. But in 8th grade I was sent back to the private school so that I would be more likely to be accepted into their high school, which I was.

The high school was all girls and very depressing as a result. Some of the most well-adjusted girls hated it. Much pressure was put on us because it was a "college preparatory school." It was hard. During my boring summers I would day-dream of boys I knew in 8th grade. (After high school I would work at summer jobs.)

My mother verbally abused me at this time. She didn't like the way I looked or acted. I was too quiet. My nose was a pug. I walked too stiffly. My hair wasn't stylish. My voice sounded funny on the telephone. And, as far as she knew, I was a lesbian. I never brought home a boy. (How could I? It was a girl's school.) When she was a teenager, she had been beautiful, dated many boys, was even guilty of petting. *She* was certainly not a lesbian. My mother was unable to accept anyone different from herself until she was in her 80's when she sat down and talked to a priest about it. She wanted to die a saint. "Get rid of your narcissism," said the priest. Which she did (I think).

Feeling terrible about myself, I would hold up in my room, studying. We had so many tests on Monday, that I had to spend all day Saturday studying and all day Sunday reviewing the material I had studied the day before. For this I was criticized harshly.

The *mean clique* in high school used to talk about me because I smelled and my hair was always greasy. This was because, like my parents, I didn't bathe often enough. My mother should have advised me to wash my hair more often at the very least. When I was 16, some girls from the *nice girls clique* took me under their wing and taught me to shower, wash my hair and set it.

Then I met a boy after a flying lesson and worked harder to keep up my appearance. My mother, seeing that I was not a lesbian after all, treated me much more kindly.

I used the infatuation on that boy to bring up my mood. I used infatuations to do that for many more years.

Everything was fine in college, only I didn't have any friends there. But there were no *mean cliques* there either. Everybody was nice. I hung around at lunch with the day-hops (girls who lived in the local area).

In 1971 on New Year's Eve I met a nice, sweet, teddy bear of a guy. I'll call him *Teddy Bear* here. He was short, muscular, overweight with long hair flying every which way. I hung on to him for 9 years until we married in 1981. I always thought he was a guarantee that I would never be alone. Still, if I became depressed, I would become infatuated with someone else and a couple of times I became involved with them.

Meanwhile, I got a good job as a computer programmer. Computer programming was a mystery to me at first. Eventually I became involved with a genius and he taught me how to program. It was easy after that and I made a good salary.

When I hit 30 I felt very old so I decided to talk Teddy Bear into marrying me. That way, my future would be assured: I would always have a friend. We got married when we were both 31.

It wasn't easy. After we were married, he became very unhappy and started spending a lot of time at the home of a single mother of 2. He said I was the source of his unhappiness but gave no reason why. As a result, of course, I became depressed and became infatuated with a smart, good-looking, alcoholic programmer at work. I had sex with him exactly once and it was not any fun. Not much later, we moved to Florida so I could work at the Kennedy Space Center. Eventually I confessed my adultery. It didn't go over well. I got Teddy Bear a job at my company delivering listings. There he met a woman I will call *Clever*. She was friendly, talkative, complimented his appearance and brought him lunch and home-made cookies. He started visiting her at night staying there until 2 AM. His excuse was that it was only temporary and it was the only thing keeping him from committing suicide. In fact he told me that he had tried suicide recently at least 3 times.

Out of my mind with worry, I let him see the girl. Also, I called his neurologist to discuss the suicide attempts. I wanted the doctor to know about it and to tell me what to do. But the girl in the office said they couldn't discuss his case with anybody else but him.

I became upset by weeks of seeing Clever and Teddy Bear to-gether. Also people started teasing me about it. And I was putting myself under too much pressure at work—teaching new pro-grammers and managing a team of them.

I couldn't stand it anymore. I was shaky and crying at work. Suddenly I flew to Maryland to be with my mother.

There I visited Ocean City, saw the DuPont houses in Delaware and saw my brothers and sisters. Then I flew back to Florida to face the same old situation.

Not long after I was back, I swung into an elation, a mania. I called Teddy Bear. He could tell from my voice that I wasn't thinking right. "Stay there. I'll be right home," he said.

I threw some clothes into a suitcase intending to stay with an acquaintance, and drove a mile to the beach. It was a lovely day—warm and sunny, not horribly hot. I watched pelicans dive for fish. Then I drove my Volkswagen up South Tropical Trail which is a scenic winding road with palm trees and beautiful homes. The date was October 1, 1984.

Recently a younger man had rejected me. Suddenly, I decided to drive into a tree at a fast rate of speed. I wanted to be reincar-nated with this man in a different time, different place. I thought, "This will hurt but it will be worth it." I sped up to 75 mph and hit the tree.

They had to use the *jaws of life* to cut me out of the car. At the hospital I was given 4 units of blood. Two tubes were put in my right lung. X-rays were done of my chest and back. The x-rays really hurt. Nothing was done for the several broken ribs I had. A screw was put into my broken right ankle.

Because my injuries were on the right side and Christ had a wound on his right side, I thought I was Jesus Christ.

A psychiatrist was called and he gave me an antipsychotic.

I thought I was okay and could go home. I pulled out my IV. Teddy Bear was told that he would have to stay with me at night to make sure I didn't pull out my chest tubes, killing myself.

The next day he called my mother and asked her to do the babysitting from now on. Mother came down to watch over me. By the time she got there I was much calmer and there was no need for her to watch me at night. She stayed in my duplex for 3 and a half months.

After about a week I was moved to the psychiatric unit. My mother brought in some casual clothes the next day. I put them on and washed my face. My fellow psychiatric patients said I looked much better.

The lung specialist was the only doctor who came to see me. The psychiatrist who had been responsible for me had gone on a 3 week vacation and had forgotten to assign a replacement. For 2 weeks the only medication I got was Extra-strength Tylenol and I was in pretty bad pain. Then I was tested and found to have had an acute psychotic break. I was given haldol, a medication they used to use in Russia to torture prisoners. It is a very distressing drug and if you have the side effects you should immediately stop taking it. It can produce lasting brain damage. I did get them to cut it in half.

Finally after 3 weeks in the unit and knowing my mother would be taking care of me, they sent me home.

I started seeing a Dr. R. who kept me on the haldol for 3 weeks although he did cut it in half. I begged him to take me off of it. When he did I plunged into a deep depression. It was horrible. There was no way to alleviate it. It was a flat, numb, pessimistic mood. Reading was impossible. Going to the beach didn't help. Nor did watching TV. My mother and I went to lunch every day and sat in the bright sunlight which helped a little. I had no energy to do anything.

A friend who was an alcoholic described the feeling this way:

When I stop drinking everything becomes bland. I get no pleasure out of anything. Nothing helps. Not TV. Not food. I just sit there and think, "So what?" Then, when I start to drink again, things go back to normal.

I was relieved to hear that at least one person in the world had the same feelings as I.

The next time I saw Dr. R., I correctly described my feelings.

"Oh, that is just the depression," he said, laughing. He prescribed a mild tranquilizer which could have worsened the depression. (But didn't.)

One day he arranged to meet me outside his office. As soon as we got to the meeting place, we had sex.

I had promised myself to move heaven and earth in order to get help for my condition. Obviously this guy had no intention of helping me. I decided to switch doctors immediately.

When I called the new doctor, Dr. C., she was puzzled as to why I would want to switch doctors in midstream. "The doctor and I agree that it would be better if I saw a woman doctor," I said. Dr. C. made an appointment to see me.

"Tell me what happened?" she said after giving me a test for depression. I was glad to tell her. No one else had ever asked before. When I told Dr. R. about it—elation followed by depression—he made up some latin sounding name for it. He was lazy as well as unethical. He didn't even try to get to the bottom of the problem. I am angry about it to this day.

Dr. C. had to try a few medications until she found one that worked. And that took weeks. This was in 1985 and the meds were not as fast acting as they are today. Nor could the doctor predict what medication would work best.

Early on I decided to choose an attitude to take towards this chronic illness. On thinking about it I had 2 choices:

(1) Continue to whine and complain.

(2) Act with the courage and dignity my father had when faced with the results of polio. He always laughed at any humiliating experiences caused by using crutches (such as falls.) When something bad happened to him he would make up a funny story about it *as it occurred.*

My father was mentally healthy. He was able to quickly accept the crippling disease and find a satisfactory way of looking at it. Then he set about comforting the young male patients in his ward. Later, he became a member of the National Foundation for Infantile Paraylsis (NFIP), the financial side of the March of Dimes. He eventually became chairman of the Baltimore Chapter.

He was proud of the way he adjusted to the braces and crutches. He could do most things an ordinary person could do: walk, ascend and descend stairs, get into and out of a car, drive a car, get up and down from a chair, get up and down from the floor, get up and down from a toilet. He could no longer dance with his wife, go on hikes, fly or go boating but he made peace with those limitations. He always had a smile on his face and was a very pleasant man. He never complained.

I decided to act like my father.

Dr. C. was pleased that I tried to follow my father's example. She said there was a strong possibility that I would be able to discontinue the meds one day. This is because I was so very nice, open-minded and never said "poor me." She said all I was lacking was *a little faith.*

Back at work, I admitted to having had a *nervous breakdown.* People were shocked. "Why did you tell us that?" they asked. They quickly lost respect for me after that.

The antidepressant still hadn't begun to work. I found it hard to think. I informed my work leader that he would have to assign me the easiest work he had.

Everyone thought my boss, the manager, was being too easy on me. In reality, though, I was disabled and should have stayed home until the medicine started to work. Dr. C. finally decided I should stay at home for a week, without pay it turned out, until I had become used to a higher dosage.

Shortly after that, the depression lifted. "I am ready to make a diagnosis," Dr. C. said. "You have manic depression."

"Oh no," I said. "Surely I don't have that. My moods may go up and down but they are within the normal range."

She reassured me that the disease was carried on the same gene as intelligence: the people who have it are more intelligent than average. Great presidents and writers have had it. "The better families have it," she said. Unfortunately I began to brag about having it. This was a real mistake.

At this time I was attending a meeting of the Separated, Widowed and Divorced (SWD), a church group. I also continued working, going to church and eating out. I begged God to make me better.

Then I met a girl who I will call *Friendly*. Every afternoon she would stop by my house. We would either talk or go to the beach. On weekend mornings we would go out for breakfast. On Saturday evenings we would go out and dance.

Friendly had a good sense of humor and would make me laugh. I wasn't over the depression yet, so this was the best thing she could have done for me.

Later, I read self-help books. This is supposed to be as helpful as cognitive therapy itself. The books suggested ways to deal with the illness. I also read spiritual books which helped me also. Some of the books were:

- *Man's Search for Meaning* by Viktor Frankl
- *Reality Therapy* by William Glasser
- *Help and Hope for Your Nerves* by Dr. Claire Weekes
- *Focusing* by Eugene T. Gendlin
- *The Road Less Travelled* by M. Scott Peck

Friendly knew a woman whose son needed a girl friend. Friendly and I agreed to meet him at a pancake breakfast. He was a good-looking 38-year-old who I will call *Handsome*. I couldn't believe he needed help finding a woman.

He was verbally abusive from the start. Soon after we met he said, "You really should grow your hair. It looks like a little kid's with those bangs. Your stomach sticks out too," he added.

A couple of months later we went out to dinner. It was a buffet and I went up to get my food. When I got back to the table, I started eating. At that moment, Handsome noticed a woman bringing her husband a roll. "Get me a roll," he ordered. I couldn't believe it. He was not crippled. He could get his own roll.

On the 20 mile drive back, he refused to talk. When we got home I said, "Are you angry?"

"Yes," he said. "The fact that you did not get me a roll shows that you are not a loving person. You also think that you are better than I because you make more money than I do. You are stuck up like I originally thought when you wore designer jeans to the pancake breakfast."

I soon found out that he had been planning to break up with me for weeks and was waiting for an excuse like this to do it. Afraid of being alone, I practically begged him on my knees to stay. So far, he had lived in my home for free. I had gotten him a job and never asked for anything in return.

Handsome decided, with some coaxing, to stay. He didn't want to have to go back to his mother.

Soon after that, he picked another fight. I made some spaghetti and forgot to drain it. He looked at it floating in a cup of water and sneered. Then he noticed a roach. (Florida is known for its' roaches.) "You love the roaches better than me," he said. "I will move out if you don't get rid of the roaches." The next day I hurried down to the hardware store and bought a green powder which effectively got rid of them.

When I told Dr. C. about this, she said, "When someone holds a gun to your head and says, 'get rid of the roaches,' don't do it." Then she told me to charge him rent. I stuck to my guns on this one and he showed me a bit more respect.

Handsome's verbal abuse began to interfere with work. To deal with the obsessive and anxious feelings I had to duck into the bathroom and do what the self-help books say to do: write what happened; what you were thinking; how it made you feel; what the reality of the situation was. Sometimes I would draw a *picture* of how the problem *felt*. Then I would meditate on it until I had found a solution to the problem or found a different way of looking at it.

This was very time consuming especially since people would hurt my feelings at work also. Mentally I was very uncomfortable—very anxious. Finally I admitted my feelings to my doctor who prescribed an anti-psychotic, which helped a lot.

Handsome and I got married in August of 1986. A few month's later, knowing I would be able to support him, he quit his job. I was infuriated. We lived in a very inexpensive house and the bills were low, it is true, but putting up with his abuse as well as having to support him was too much.

Partly because I was so angry, we no longer got along at all. He started threatening to move out.

I was one of the few laid off from work after the Challenger accident. The layoffs occurred in 1987. As soon as I was laid off I went to Human Resources and told them that my boss was prejudiced against me because I was going to a psychiatrist. After a little investigation, they got me my job back. But not long after that, my boss called a meeting and asked each programmer to document any mistakes I made.

Programmers make mistakes all the time. They spend most of their day correcting them. But H.R. doesn't know this and would take seriously any list of mistakes I made.

I started doing things on my own. I went to Weight Watchers and lost 10 pounds. I took a painting class and began to paint respectable watercolors. We had bought a sail boat so I took sailing lessons. I went to group therapy.

In March of 1988 my boss decided to transfer me. He said that everyone agreed that I was slow and made mistakes. He wanted me to go to a non-programming group. I told him everyone makes mistakes and are not punished for it. Programming was the only thing I knew how to do.

"You would be better off out of here," he said.

That evening I meditated on it. My boss was right, I decided. I might end up working for a much nicer person.

The next day, I was transferred—to a small programming group. Under a little pressure by the new boss, I relearned how to quickly solve problems. It was a group of 5 very nice guys who would not have been upset if I had told them I had bipolar disorder. (Which I didn't. I had learned my lesson.)

In February of 1989, Handsome moved all of his books to his mother's house. He spent many nights at her house staying away for a week sometimes. His mother had an apartment built in her basement for him. Still, I was afraid to be alone.

Around this time, I met an unhappily married man at work who I will call *Gentle*.

He told me he looked forward to coming to work because of me.

One day he handed me a piece of paper on which he confessed his love for me. "I feel the same way," I said. He smiled with relief. He told me that the next time his wife threatened divorce he would say, "Go ahead." He said we would not have to wait long. The following Monday his wife threatened divorce. He told her to go ahead. His wife stormed out and went away for 2 weeks.

Given the green light, I called Handsome and asked him to move out. He was a little shaken by this but was more cheerful by the time I rented a truck for him and helped him move. (A year or two later Handsome called me. His mother wanted to kick him out so he called me seeking a place to stay. I told him I was happily married and he quickly ended the conversation).

Gentle and I got married in May of 1990. Our marriage was much happier than my other marriages had been. However I still was very afraid of being alone. I was also still very sensitive to criticism by my husband or anyone else for that matter.

After a few years, my job became more complicated and I was not able to keep up with it. I became very very nervous and my therapist said it was okay to take more klonopin, an anti-anxiety drug. Because of taking this, I became rather groggy and depressed. Dr. G. (Dr. C. had retired) ordered me to take less of the drug but pressure at work began to build. I started feeling as if my head was going to burst. In October of 1995 my husband took me to see Dr. G. The doctor urged me to go on disability.

"Probably no one works there who is as sick as you are. Also many people on disability are not as sick as you are. Some bipolar people have jobs, it is true, but they have much easier jobs. You have very low self-esteem. If somebody at work says something you don't like, you might possibly commit suicide. Bring me the disability forms and I will fill them out for you."

Later Dr. G. said that now that I was under less stress, there was a possibility of remission for several years. "Maybe we can try getting you off medication altogether."

I never expected him to say that. Psychiatric medications had come a long way. He prided himself on being an expert on them.

The rest is from my journal:

> **10/96** on disability from work. becoming anxious about not having a job. feel guilty. Because of anxiety and depression, Dr. G. changed my medication and put me into a hospital out-patient group. It helped.

> **1/97** Attended a Women Entering New Directions (WENDI) class. Took a test and discovered that I was an introvert in every way. Realized that I had made many good choices during my life which had prepared me for writing my book (about Theodore Roosevelt). Only an introvert would enjoy all the research that required. Started a volunteer job at the hospital gift shop.

8/97 Heard a woman in the gift shop talking about me. Felt very bad.

12/97 Dr. G. says I am fully functional now. I only have to see him quarterly.

1/27/98 Had a mystical experience unlike anything I had ever experienced before. I thought it must have been God. Because of that, I resolved from that time forward to never commit a sin, no matter how small. I also decided to always do the right thing whenever called upon to do it.

1/28/98 My decision to "do no wrong" was tested and I passed but was outraged at who tempted me.

2/5/98 still upset

2/10/98 I am obsessing over it.

2/14/98 I am blowing it up out of proportion.

2/17/98 Outraged....

Sometime after this, I became quite calm nearly all of the time. After a few years the paranoia around other people no longer hurt. In 2002, I walked into a room where several people were talking about me. My only thought was, "What they are saying is true, but who cares what they think?" From that point on people were no longer able to hurt me. This is probably because my self-esteem had risen because of the WENDI class. Depression and anxiety are no longer a problem. However, I still take medication.

3

Cognitive Therapy

Mental health is dedication to reality at all costs.—M. Scott Peck, *The Road Less Travelled*

Change the way you think and your reactions will change.—Dr. Claire Weekes, *Help and Hope for Your Nerves*

Those of us who are neurotic, believe that we are somehow to blame for all our problems. If a relative in another state commits suicide, we feel guilty because we should have called her more often. If a friend dies a natural death, we should have spent more time with her. If our mother visits us and has a stroke, we feel we must have pushed her too much. If our hair looks bad we think that *we* look bad. If we can't immediately program a remote it is because we are stupid. If our child gets a bad grade it is because we are bad parents.

Our feelings get hurt too easily. We can't handle criticism. If we are verbally abused, we are struck silent. If our spouse is depressed, it is our fault.

Other problems we may have are perfectionism, obsessions, compulsions, panic attacks, fear, dependency, approval addiction, agoraphobia, anxiety and procrastination.

This is a real problem and is known as *wrong thinking*. And we *should* seek help for it. Also, as Dr. Claire Weekes wrote, "There must be no self pity. And this means *no self pity*." [1]

We must change our thinking in order to improve our moods. Situations do not make us feel bad. It is our *thinking* about the situation that causes our emotions. [2]

Depressed people tend to think of themselves as inadequate, unattractive, unpopular and inferior. They are completely unable to look at situations realistically. [3] The goal of cognitive therapy is to gain "lasting changes in your mood, outlook and productivity, " says Dr. Burns who wrote *Feeling Good, The New Mood Therapy*. He says that studies have shown that cognitive therapy may change brain chemistry and the structure of the brain itself. He also believes that bibliotherapy—reading a good self-help book such as his own, may be as helpful as psychotherapy and medications for depression. [4]

Dr. Burns agrees with other medical doctors that mood-stabilizers such as lithium or valproic acid (Depakene) are necessary for bipolar disorder. Nevertheless, cognitive therapy, he says, goes a long way towards helping bipolar patients. [5]

Kay Redfield Jamison also believes that psycotherapy helps. She says, "One of the ultimate goals of doing psychotherapy with manic-depressive patients might be to permit lower levels of lithium, thereby minimizing the cognitive, temperamental, and other side effects of the drug." [6]

Dr. Burns says, "Evidence is mounting that a combination of medication and psychotherapy provides the best help for most patients with depression." He adds that family education improves the outcome of bipolar disorder. He says, "Eventually, I gave up treating patients with drugs alone." [7] He also noticed that practicing self-help between sessions helps to hasten recovery. [8]

Changing your thoughts

You can change your thoughts. For example you can change, "I hate public speaking" to "Public speaking is a challenge but I'm working on it." [9] Negative thoughts are almost always not based on reality. The self-help books suggest writing when something upsetting happens. Write what happened; if you want to, write how you felt; write what you were thinking; write the reality of the situation.

Dr. Burns gives the example of a mother and daughter accidently taking a train with no amenities. The mother was thirsty. The daughter *thought*, "Mother has been walking around all day and because she didn't understand the train schedule, she's thirsty. I'm a terrible daughter." The daughter *felt*—guilt. The *reality* is the daughter had tried her best to explain the train schedule to her mother and her mother had misunderstood. It is not the daughter's fault that the mother misunderstood.

Another example:

What happened—A teacher told a mother that her child was doing poorly in school. The mother was a very sensitive person.

The mother *thought*—I am a bad mother. I should have helped my child with his school work.

The *reality* of the situation—"I am not a bad mother….Maybe I can work with him and his teacher and find out how to help him…." [10]

Dr. Islett, who wrote *Think Right, Feel Right, The Building Block Guide For Happiness and Emotional Well-Being*, suggests replacing an unhealthy thought with a healthy one.

For example:

Unhealthy thought—Someone said my hair looks bad today. I never look good.

Healthy thought—I have difficult hair but I have a pretty smile which makes up for it.

Unhealthy thought—I played tennis badly today. I'll never be good at this.

Healthy thought—Becoming a good tennis player will take time and practice, and I guess I should accept the fact that I will mishit the ball a lot, especially in the beginning.

Unhealthy thought—I'll never get this new remote to work.
Healthy thought—I'll probably get the remote to work. I'll just have to read the directions.

Unhealthy thought—The children are irritating.
Healthy thought—They are just being children and having fun. [11]

Unhealthy thought—If I do something for someone, they should thank me.
Healthy thought—If I do help someone they are likely to be grateful but they are not obligated to say thank you or even feel grateful. Why expect it? [12]

Unhealthy thought—I am a loser. I got a low grade on a test.
Healthy thought—If I do not do well in this course, which is unlikely since I am a good student, I can take another course or switch to another major. [13]

Specific problems we may have

Need for total acceptance

Dr. Burns gives the example of a musician who wants to be the greatest musician in the world.

Unhealthy thought—I am not the greatest musician.
Healthy thought—Many people like my music.

Unhealthy thought—But *everybody* doesn't like my music. How can I enjoy my music if I know I am not the greatest?

Healthy thought—I can enjoy it by playing music that I love. [14]

Perfectionism

Perfection doesn't exist. According to Dr. Burns, we need to lower our standards. Set time limits for an activity and stop when the time is up. For example play the piano for only an hour.

When Dr. Burns first began running, he could only run 200-300 yards because it was very hilly country. The next day his goal was to run *less* than the day before. He was always able to do this. He had accomplished his goal and felt good about it. Eventually, he found himself running more and more and worked himself up to 7 miles. He advises choosing any activity and aiming for 40% instead of 100%. It will be much more enjoyable that way. He says resolve to do things less than perfectly. [15]

Obsessions

Accept your obsessions and live with them for the time being. We cannot force them to go away. [16] "Do not make the mistake of believing that there are certain thoughts you must not think, dare not think, as if there are parts of your brain you must not use," says Dr. Weekes author of *Hope and Help for Your Nerves.* [17]

Procrastination

Procrastination causes lack of motivation and lowers your self-esteem. Do something, anything, to help yourself.

First of all, get organized. Make a daily, hour by hour schedule if necessary. Be sure to break complex tasks into smaller tasks while making a to-do list. You can base the smaller tasks on how long they will take. Allot some time for each one and stop at the alloted time. Don't wait until you are in the mood to do something. Do a little at a time no matter what your mood. [18]

Panic attacks

The dread of panic attacks may bring them on. [19] Dr. Weeks says panic attacks consist of 2 fears. The first fear is the actual situation you are afraid of, such as feeling trapped while you are in a church surrounded by people. The second fear is the one where you think you'll make a fool of yourself in front of all those people. Focus on the first fear and let it pass. Forget about the second fear. Eventually panic attacks will become a thing of the past. [20]

Agoraphobia

Dr. Weeks says that, "Agoraphobia…[is the] fear of leaving the safety of home, either alone or in the company of others." She suggests leaving the house anyway, and walking to the store. *Accept* the people you run into and listen to them if they want to talk. At first you'll be thinking, "What if they never stop talking." Don't worry. They will. Keep reminding yourself of that. [21]

Criticism and verbal abuse

When anyone is criticized, it triggers negative thoughts. This is normal. If handling this by writing, identify your negative and illogical thoughts. Write down the reality of the situation. And consider if the person was right or wrong.

If the person is still present, get to the bottom of the situation by asking questions. If you disagree with this person, don't argue. Try to find a grain of truth in their statement. Then, explain your position while admitting you might be wrong. [22]

Dependency

Dr. Burns reassures us that we "have the capacity to feel happy when [we] are alone." You don't have to share every activity with someone. You should plan fun activities to do when alone.

He gives the example of a patient, a teenage girl, who had moved to a new town. She had no friends. She spent all her time, at home, studying. She'd say, "If only I was part of the in-crowd and had a boyfriend I'd be happy." Dr. Burns told her to start going out alone to do the things she enjoyed. She started going to art shows and concerts and found out she was having a good time. Her mood and self-confidence improved and she developed a network of friends. [23]

Dealing with a whiner

When dealing with a whiner, find some way to agree with them. For example say, "That *is* a problem." They will run out of steam if you agree with them. [24]

Guilt

My father felt guilty when his friend, Hubert, committed suicide in 1932 when they were both 22. Hubert had called him and asked how my father's uncle had committed suicide. My father explained:

The maid said he ate breakfast and played with his dog. He seemed to be okay. He said he was going out to clean his cars.
The garage door was closed. After 3 hours, the maid went to check on him. He was sitting in his car, dead. There was a strong odor of carbon monoxide. We knew it was suicide even though the coroner said it was accidental.

The very next day, Hubert killed himself in the same manner and my father felt terribly guilty. He thought that if he had not told that story, Hubert would still be alive. He should have realized that Hubert's curiosity was odd and that something must be wrong. If only he had asked Hubert if everything was okay.

The reality of the situation was that my father never *could* predict the future. The only things he could predict were from past experience such as the Beatles' music would become elevator music (to our horror). If he had known his friend was going to commit suicide he would have tried to prevent it. But he couldn't have known. Suicidal people even fool their psychiatrists.

If you have found that you *did* make a mistake, admit it to yourself, try to fix it if possible and learn from it. Try not to do it again.

Dr. Weekes says, "If your own actions have disgraced you, you have no alternative but to study where you have failed and be determined not to do so again." [25]

4

Alcoholics Anonymous (A.A.)

I'll never forget the first time I met Bill Wilson. I was a couple of months sober and so excited, so thrilled to actually meet the co-founder that I gushed all over him with what my sobriety meant to me and my undying gratitude for his starting A.A. When I ran down, he took my hand in his and said simply, "Pass it on." — from a letter to the A.A. General Service Office

Using some ideas she got while listening to a sermon, Anne Copely decided to change her thoughts in order to change her behavior. She made up 10 rules. Four were from the sermon. The rest she made up herself. She read them several times a day and often thought about them.

She was bipolar and her only goal was to become normal, an attainable goal. As a result she became much better than normal and claims to have been cured of bipolar disorder.

Anne's rules

1. I am made in the image of God; therefore, I am worthwhile.
2. What I think is what I will become.
3. I can visualize the person I want to be; and today I will think and behave like that person.

4. Just for today, I will love others and think of them before myself.
5. Just for today, I will do something for someone else.
6. Today, I will not think of things that scare me.
7. Today, I will not talk unnecessarily, so that what I do say will be important.
8. Today, I will do three things that need to be done.
9. Today, I will not worry about things I cannot change.
10. Today, I will not allow my environment to determine my happiness.

These rules contain one of the philosophies of A.A. *one step at a time thinking* rather than changing your whole life *forever*. [1]

Hazeldon

My sister, Sue, became an alcoholic because 2 of our aunts drank "like fishes" and she thought it was glamorous. They were sophisticated, beautiful and funny.

She used to drink with a friend named Jamie. Jamie had lost a lot of business because of his drinking and decided to do something about it. He went to Hazeldon, an addiction treatment center. After he got back, he invited her over. "I don't have any alcohol in the house, but I can offer you coffee," he said. She said that was fine. So he went into the kitchen to make it. He took his time. On the coffee table was literature about A.A. and Hazeldon which she read. She took to going there once or twice a week. There was always new reading material on the coffee table.

One day she felt very nervous and went to the local bar to get a strong drink. It didn't help. She then went to a diner and then went home. She felt very uncomfortable. She felt like she didn't belong there.

She called Jamie and said, "I want what you *have*." He said, "Pack a bag; I'll make arrangements and come get you. He drove her to his house. "We are going to Hazeldon," he said. "My mother will drive us to the airport."

Once on the airplane he said, "They are going to ask you if you want a drink. Have a martini." She said, "No. I want to give up drinking!" He said, "Order one and enjoy it. *It's the last drink you will ever have.*"

Hazeldon has a 70% success rate. She went to 3 lectures a day, took personality tests, psychological tests, did assigned reading and received help from priests, nuns and rehabilitated alcoholics. It was a 12 Step program. Step 5 was to tell a trusted person everything you've done wrong in your life. She confided in a monk who was also a priest. He gave her absolution. Step 9 had her apologize to the people she had harmed. Step 12 was to forget yourself and help other people which she tries to do.

When the people at Hazelton felt she was well enough, they sent her to a halfway house in Arlington, VA. She got a job and stayed there for 6 weeks. Then she went home.

She hasn't had a drink since.

Bill Wilson

I myself have never been addicted to alcohol. I don't like the way it makes me feel—dizzy and unable to keep my balance. I need more control of my body than that. And I am a quiet person. Liquor only makes me quieter.

A man named Bill Wilson had a drinking problem and his story fills me with awe. He had some mental health problems too—panic attacks and recurring depression which alcohol partially relieved. When Bill was 20, he was offered a beer. That didn't have much effect on him but the next day he was offered a mixed drink and got "thoroughly drunk, and within the next time or two [he] passed out completely."

Bill became a stock speculator and had some success. His constant drinking ruined both his business and his reputation. [2]

By 1930 he was on a downhill slope. He wrote promises to his wife in the family Bible and in letters that he would never drink again. But he couldn't give it up.

In 1933 he went to Towns Hospital, a facility for treating alcoholics. Dr. William D. Silkworth, the doctor who ran the hospital told him that he believed alcoholism was a legitimate illness. The healthy individual does not have the same craving for alcohol that alcoholics have. [3]

In 1934 Bill went on a binge after being offered one free drink. In November his phone rang. It was his friend Ebby T. Bill invited him over. He offered Ebby pineapple juice and gin. Ebby drank only the pineapple juice and Bill asked why. "I've got religion," Ebby said. "I no longer drink." He had joined the Oxford Group and admitted he was hopeless, made restitution and tried to practice unselfish giving. [4] "I learned that I had to admit I was licked; I learned that I ought to take stock of myself and confess my defects to another person in confidence; I learned that I needed to make restitution for the harm I had done others. I was told that I ought to practice the kind of giving that has no price tag on it, the giving of yourself to somebody...they taught me that I should try to pray to whatever God I thought there was for the power to carry out these simple precepts....If I did not believe there was any God, then I had better try the experiment of praying to whatever God there *might* be." [5]

Bill could not get Ebby's message out of his head. He continued to drink however. He turned up drunk at an Oxford Group meeting where he met Dr. Sam Shoemaker. Ebby, seeing that Bill was drunk, offered him a plate of beans. Bill was excited about the group but continued to drink. [6]

He soon realized he was helpless against his addiction to alcohol and signed himself into Dr. Silkworth's hospital. After the alcohol wore off, Bill fell into a very bad depression. He felt there was nothing left for him but death or madness. He was at the *jumping-off place.*

Bill was an atheist so he prayed, "If there be a God, let Him show Himself!" Suddenly he had a religious experience. He saw a white light, a mountain and felt a wind "not of air, but of spirit." This, he felt, must be God. He felt ecstasy and remained in that state for some time.

Bill had just turned 39. The minute his wife, Lois, saw him, "she knew something overwhelming had happened…[his] whole being expressed hope and joy." [7]

One Sunday, the Group asked him to speak. After he spoke, a man came up to him and remarked about how much Bill knew about alcoholics. Bill invited the man to meet him and a few other members at a nearby cafeteria. Bill found that he could do little to cure this man's alcohol problem. [8] He tried to cure other alcoholics also.

"Stop preaching at them," Dr. Silkworth said, "and give them the hard medical facts first. This may soften them up at depth so that they will be willing *to do anything* to get well. Then they may accept those spiritual ideas of yours, and even a higher power." [9]

One day Bill had an overwhelming urge to drink. The only possible help for him, he felt, was to talk to another alcoholic. He made a few calls and tracked down a woman who said, "I know just the man for you. He is a doctor. We all call him 'Dr. Bob'…. Bob has tried so hard; I know he wants to stop. He has tried medical cures, he has tried various religious approaches, including the Oxford Groups. He has tried with all his will, but somehow he cannot seem to do it." [10] She introduced Bill to Dr. Bob.

Silkworth had encouraged Bill to stop preaching at alcoholics. Talk to them as one alcoholic to another. Tell them that alcoholism is a physical disease, not a moral one. Bill talked to Dr. Bob. He played down the Oxford Group and the religious experiences. [11] The date June 10, 1935 is considered to be the date A.A. first began. It is the date on which Bill helped his first alcoholic, Dr. Bob Smith, to recover. [12] During the summer of 1935 Bill and Dr. Bob had long discussions about how to reach alcoholics and help them recover. Dr. Silkworth had already taught them that alcoholism was a disease of the body and not a sin. But it could destroy the soul. [13] They got some of their other ideas straight from the Oxford Groups—"self-examination, acknowledgement of character defects, restitution for harm done, and working with others...." [14] Bill wanted to form a group which would be tailor-made for alcoholics only. The Oxford Groups were for anyone in trouble, not just alcoholics.

Also, the Oxford Groups were too evangelical. Alcoholics couldn't take the pressure to serve God. And their concepts of absolute purity, honesty, unselfishness and love were too much to push on alcoholics. [15] They did feel it was necessary to take an inventory of their faults and confide in a person whom they trust. In 1949 Bill took his 5th Step and told his friend Father Dowling every mistake he had made in his life.

Bill and Dr. Bob discussed the necessity of helping others so that they could stay sober themselves; how important it was for one alcoholic to explain their theories to another alcoholic; how important it was to set past relationships right; to ask for strength from God at least daily; attend weekly meetings; help other alcoholics. [16]

One of their friends, Roland H., had been to Carl Jung. He asked Dr. Jung to cure him of his alcoholism. Dr. Jung said there was no medical or psychiatric cure for alcoholism. Roland H. asked if there was anything else that might help him. Jung replied, "There [is] provided [you] could become the subject of a spiritual or religious experience—in short, a genuine conversion." He cautioned that such experiences were relatively rare. He said, "Place [yourself] in a religious atmosphere and hope for the best."

Roland H. joined the Oxford Group and did have a conversion experience and stopped drinking as a result. [17]

The founders of A.A., Bill Wilson and Dr. Bob Smith, knew that the members would have to depend upon a higher power to be cured of their drinking problem. They needed to experience God in a truly personal way which would make it possible for them to have the mystical experience that was so necessary for a real cure. New members had to start out by asking for God's help. After their religious experience, or conversion, they would stop asking God for what *they* wanted and start asking Him what *He* wanted them to do. [18]

The Serenity Prayer

The Serenity Prayer was in an obituary which said, "Mother— God grant me the serenity to accept the things I cannot change, courage to change the things I can, and the wisdom to know the difference Goodbye."

Bill's secretary copied it and used it in her letters to members. The prayer is said at every A.A. meeting. It is credited to Reinhold Niebuhr, a 20th century theologian who got it from an 18th century theologian. [19]

The Twelve Steps

Bill wrote the 12 Steps at home, in bed. He wasn't feeling well. He prayed, then rapidly began writing. He thought there should be 12 steps because there were 12 disciples and he thereafter stuck to this number.

A caller that evening objected to his frequent references to God. [20] "There is too much God in it and too much getting down on their knees. Bill you've got to tune it down. If it is too religious it won't work." [21]

Bill said later, "In Step Two we decided to describe God as a 'Power greater than ourselves.' In Step Three and Eleven, we inserted the words 'God as we understand Him.'" They deleted the words "on our knees" from Step 7. The lead in sentence to the Steps became "Here are the Steps we took which are *suggested* as a Program of Recovery…." These steps were to be suggestions only. [22]

Later they took the 12 Steps to a large Buddhist monastery. The priest looked them over and said, "Why these are fine!" They didn't believe in God as Jews and Christians did, but since it referred to God as you understand him they said, "That certainly clears up the point for us. Yes A.A.'s Twelve Steps will certainly be accepted by the Buddhists around here." [23]

Bill went through the worst depression in his life in 1944 and it lasted 11 years. Mary M. said, "It was awful. There were long periods of time when he couldn't get out of bed. He just stayed in bed, and Lois would see that he ate. An awful lot of people believed he was drinking. That was one of the worst rumors we had within A.A." Even so, He did a lot of work during that time. He wrote *Twelve Steps and Twelve Traditions*. [24]

Twelve Traditions

Bill decided to create some guidelines for the groups to follow. He decided to call them Traditions. Some of them are explained here:

Anonymity

A famous baseball player claimed to be a member of A.A. He got a lot of publicity for A.A. [25] Even so, Bill finally decided he he did not want any member to become rich and famous based on their A.A. membership. Most people crave the limelight. Bill thought this was an unhealthy tendency. It was alright to get publicity for A.A. but not okay to get it for themselves.

The only purpose of the individual group was to carry its message to the alcoholic who still needs help. Once alcoholics see that A.A. has only one purpose, they will be more inclined to seek help. [26]

Inclusiveness

At first, AA's were unsure of who to accept into their groups. They thought they would have more success with those who had hit bottom and were desperate enough to pray to God. But many alcoholics were suffering *without* having lost everything.

The groups were also concerned that they might attract riff-raff. Finally, they decided to accept anyone who had "a sincere desire to stop drinking." [27]

Publicity

A.A.'s work needed to be publicized but the press had to come to them. They were not to go out and seek publicity themselves. Also, the press could not use their real names. Jack Alexander, a writer for the *Saturday Evening Post* wrote an article that was published in their March 1, 1941 issue. It had tremendous impact. A.A. was swamped with orders for *Alcoholics Anonymous* (their big book). [28] Finally, A.A. had the attention of the nation. [29]

Self-supporting

In 1940 John D. Rockefeller, Jr. gave a dinner for A.A. He invited 400 people. Only a fraction showed up but they were very rich and could have donated millions to A.A. But Nelson Rockefeller said, "[A.A.'s] power lies in the fact that one member carries the good message to the next without any thought of financial income or reward. Therefore, it is our belief that Alcoholics Anonymous should be self-supporting so far as money is concerned. It needs only our goodwill." [30]

He gave them a few thousand to tide them over but not the millions they had been expecting. "A.A. stayed poor," Bill said.

Someone left A.A. some money in their will. A.A. decided they ought to turn it down. One of their traditions became "Every A.A. group ought to be fully self-supporting, declining outside contributions."

Nonprofessional

Bill thought he'd make a good alcoholic therapist but it was decided that A.A. would remain nonprofessional. It would be okay to employ needed workers though. The first one was a janitor who insisted on a salary even though he was to be given free room and board.

Bill Wilson and Dr. Bob Smith had spent their entire time on A.A. and had not earned a penny. [31] It was decided that the royalties from their books should go to them. Also, each A.A. group would contribute towards office expenses. Finally A.A. was self-supporting. Since that time A.A. has refused all outside contributions. [32]

Some of Bill and Dr. Bob's books are *Alcoholics Anonymous, Alcoholics Anonymous Comes of Age, Twelve Steps and Twelve Traditions*, and *The A.A. Way of Life (As Bill Sees It)*. [33]

Public controversy

The groups are not allowed to discuss controversial topics. They should never discuss religion, politics or economics except when they are outside of the group and not speaking as an A.A. member. [34]

Therapeutic value of A.A.

Harry M. Tiebout, M.D. wrote, "The success of the group with any alcoholic depends upon the degree to which the individual goes through a conversion or spiritual activation…[which is] succeeded by a feeling of peace, serenity, and the profound conviction that he was freed from the bondage of liquor."

He said that 10% of alcoholics experience a sudden conversion. The remaining 90% achieve the same results gradually, by following the Steps. [35]

5

Conversion

We had to find a power by which we could live, and it had to be a power <u>greater than ourselves</u>.—Bill W.—*Alcoholics Anonymous*

Your higher power

When I want to be comforted I think of the way my parents, deceased now, put me to bed when I was 3. They smiled down on me with loving and total acceptance. Their unconditional acceptance of me was *love* and I remember feeling it. Tolstoy said, "He who has love has God in him, and is in God—because God is Love." (*What Men Live By*, Leo Tolstoy)

I used to keep this *Prayer of Saint Francis of Assisi* in my desk. I would open my desk drawer whenever necessary and read the prayer:

Lord, make me an instrument of Your peace,
Where there is hatred, let me sow love,
Where there is doubt, faith,
Where there is despair, hope,
Where there is darkness, light,
And where there is sadness, joy.
O Divine Master, grant that I may not so much need to be consoled, as to console;

To be understood, as to understand;
To be loved, as to love;
For it is in giving that we receive—
It is in pardoning that we are pardoned;
And it is in dying that we are born to eternal life.

Occasionally I would put some water from Lourdes on my forehead and ask to be healed. (Lourdes water is from a spring in France. It is supposed to have healing properties.)

Alcoholics Anonymous members (A.A.'s) must put their faith in a higher power in order to get well.

Captain Al Haynes, the hero of the crash of United Flight 232 in 1989 referred to *luck* in a speech he gave in the 1990's. Luck may have been Al Haynes higher power:

First of all...just getting the plane on the ground was a tremendous piece of luck....
Another piece of luck was where we were...we were over the relative flatlands over Iowa....
The weather was an amazing piece of luck...if we'd try to control this DC-10 under any kind of turbulence, we'd never had made it....
The time of day was also very advantageous...it was day, we could see what we were trying to find...[also] it was right at shift-change time for the hospitals...so they were double shifted for our arrival....
And the last piece of luck...it was Wednesday, the one day of the month when the Air National Guard at Sioux City was on duty, and 285 trained National Guardsmen were at the airport, waiting for us, when we got there.... In 1987 the National Guard "had a drill, they pretended a wide-body aircraft crashed on the same runway" as United Flight 232. They had corrected the weaknesses in their emergency plan and were well prepared. [1]

President Dwight D. Eisenhower spoke of his luck that he was "born an American." [2] *We* were lucky he was born here.

Sudden Conversion

God "comes to most men gradually" [3] but here I will talk about sudden conversion rather than gradual conversion because that is what I experienced.

William James said:

> *It is natural for those who have a sudden conversion to think of it as being a miracle rather than a natural process. Voices are often heard, lights seen, or visions witnessed; automatic phenomena occur; and it always seems, after the surrender of the personal will, as if an extraneous higher power had flooded in and taken possession.* [4]

James also says:

> *If the fruits for life of the state of conversion are good, we ought to idealize and venerate it, even though it be a piece of natural psychology; if not, we ought to make short work with it, no matter what supernatural being may have infused it.* [5]

Results of sudden conversion

An alcoholic said, "From that hour drink has had no terrors for me. I never touch it, never want it." [6]

A man who had been severely depressed said, "From this day onwards a new interior life began for me: not that my melancholy has disappeared, but it had lost its sting." [7]

One person said, "My soul enjoyed sweet peace." [8]

S. H. Hadley "became an active and useful rescuer of drunkards in New York." [9]

Henry Alline "became a Christian minister, and thence forward his life was fit to rank for its austerity and single-mindedness with that of the most devoted saints." [10]

M. Ratisbonnne "gave up his project of marriage, became a priest [and] founded a mission of nuns...." [11]

Clifford Beers said, "The thousands of false impressions recorded during the seven hundred and ninety-eight days of my depression seemed at once to correct themselves." [12]

Anne de Guigne who at age 4 was "a most tempestuous little person...a little tyrant" became unselfish and devoted herself to the well being of other children. [13]

A "satanic figure" during World War II, a Nazi who killed every psychotic person he could get his hands on, became a sympathetic counselor and "lived up to the highest moral standard" while imprisoned in Russia after the war. [14]

Bill W. who helped found Alcoholics Anonymous, had a "sudden and profound" conversion. Alarmed, He called his doctor to ask if he was crazy. The doctor, who later discovered that this type of experience was not uncommon, said, "Something has happened to you I don't understand. But you had better hang on to it. Anything is better than the way you were." [15]

St. Francis of Assisi was the leader of a gang that terrorized the city. He spent time in jail. Later he came to notice the poverty in his town and began to pray and give money to the poor. He left the town and saw a broken down church in the countryside.

He heard a voice saying, "Francis, restore my Church, which is falling into ruins." He founded an order of monks. [16]

St. Camillus De Lellis was a soldier with a gambling addiction. After his conversion he founded a Congregation of Nursing Brothers. He had them wear a Red Cross on their shoulder. His Brothers became the beginning of all later Red Cross movements. [17]

St. Vincent De Paul was a man who looked forward to ecclesiastical rank and showed signs of temper and dark moods. After his conversion he no longer cared about rank or money. He became good, lovable and kind. He dedicated himself to the welfare of children, priests and nuns. [18]

Matt Talbot had been a very troublesome boy. At 12 he went to work in a store that sold liquor. At 13 he came home drunk. At 27, still an alcoholic, he found that he had spent all his money on drink. After his conversion he never took another drink. His bad habits of cursing, theft and lying disappeared. He was always cheerful. [19]

My grandfather, an atheist, was sick in the hospital with encephalomyelitis and pleurisy. Encephalomyelitis is a virus which causes inflammation of the brain and spinal cord. Pleurisy is a painful inflammation of the lining of the lungs which makes breathing difficult. Because of the pleurisy he was in constant pain. He was "at the end of my rope." In great pain he said, "God, if there is a God, please help me." Suddenly he felt a spiritual presence. He said to his wife, "I want the priest to come." He converted to Catholicism after that.

I had a conversion also. I was with a group of women, thinking about how kind and helpful they all were. I felt connected to them in some way. Suddenly I was surrounded by an atmosphere of which I was a part. It was a very comfortable and pleasant experience, a little like floating in a warm ocean. Within seconds it was over and my body once again felt separate, alone and a little uncomfortable.

I thought the *atmosphere* was God. From then on I decided to do no wrong, no matter how small and harmless the sin was. I also decided to do whatever right thing I was called upon to do.

This promise stayed with me. It was a permanent change in my thinking. Also, a calmness descended upon me, little noticed at first, but soon it was strong and was with me all the time. We who have bipolar disorder know that calmness will go a long way towards healing our brain. I was able to judge myself more realistically and my self-esteem improved almost right away. As a result of that, the paranoia, after a time, stopped hurting. No longer did I feel self-destructive when someone insulted me. I have not had depression, paranoia or an anxiety attack since and it has been at least fifteen years.

6

Mental Health

You may of course ask whether we really need to refer to "saints." Wouldn't it suffice just to refer to decent people? It is true that they form a minority. More than that, they always will remain a minority. And yet I see therein the very challenge to join the minority. For the world is in a bad state, but everything will become still worse unless each of us does his best.—Viktor E. Frankl, *Man's Search for Meaning*

The goal of this book is to show the reader steps he or she can take to become mentally healthy. The healthy person is no longer narcissistic—self-absorbed. They are less self-conscious than most people. Their neuroses are a shadow of what they used to be. Their self-esteem is realistic. They are mature, no longer paralyzed by fear, and they are calmer than almost anyone around them.

Mentally healthy people are in the minority but mental health *is* an attainable goal.

It is to our advantage that we have suffered. Someone who has a good job, who can afford to buy many things, who is rarely sick or in pain and is prominent in the community has no reason to work on self-improvement. Not until they get sick or lose their job or get divorced do they realize that maybe they have been doing something wrong. Not until then do they work on self-improvement, pray, and seek help from other human beings.

That is the only road to mental health—the road that I've tried to explain in this book. Our aim is a possible one.

Out of curiosity I decided to study self-actualization. Self-actualized people are very rare. It is doubtful that you have ever seen one. You have to be mentally healthy first in order to achieve it. Once we achieve mental health we can try to imitate the self-actualized. We can do this by reading about them, or if we ever knew one, remembering what they were like.

Self-Actualization was a term invented by Abraham H. Maslow of Brandeis University to describe the most mentally healthy of human beings. All their needs having been met, they are at ease, un-self-conscious, funny, do not care what other people think and are comfortable in their own skins. Their purpose in life is usually something to do with helping others. Maslow says Lincoln and Jefferson were very likely self-actualized people. They are the only 2 in history that he could label with assurance. Using them as examples he went about befriending others who seemed to him to be self-actualized. (They refused to be formerly studied.)

Lest you think that only great presidents become self-actualized, I want to reassure you that quite ordinary people do as well. Although I may be prejudiced, I believe my father, a Baltimore businessman, was a self-actualized man. He handled his leg paralysis bravely. He helped others who had been disabled by polio. He had most of the qualities described in this chapter: accepted himself; accepted reality; was simple and natural; was not a clothes horse; was a man of integrity; liked solitude; was able to remain stable when faced with grave misfortune; was friendly to people regardless of race or religion; felt kinship with most human beings.

My younger brother agrees. He wrote several months ago:

> *Dad personified integrity....He was comfortable in his own skin...[he was] at peace with himself. Never complaining, he almost always wore a smile....I think Dad*

was a genuinely good man. Though he didn't practice any religion, he was a man of high ethical caliber exemplifying responsibility, honesty, work ethic, humility, patience, discipline, fairness, fortitude, good humor, respect and kindness. Although a man of few words, those he spoke were never words of complaint or criticism. On the contrary he would often try to lighten things up or diffuse a potential argument.

Self-actualized People

Self-actualized people fully use their talents. They appear to "be doing the best they can." Their basic needs have been met. These include the need for safety, belonging, love, respect and self-respect. Their cognitive needs for knowledge and understanding have been met. They have established a philosophy of life. [1]

What follows are the characteristics of self-actualized people as discovered by Abraham Maslow. After each characteristic I have included quotes from Abraham Lincoln's acquaintances, friends and biographers to illustrate the point:

1. More Efficient Perception of Reality

They see reality clearly and are better at predicting the future as a result. Maslow says that the neurotic's thoughts about a situation are, as we have already seen, "cognitively *wrong.*" Self-actualized people can cope with chaos better than normal. They are logical.

They "judge people correctly and efficiently." [2]

Lincoln:

Lincoln's friend Josua Speed wrote:

He always resolved every question into its primary elements and gave up every point on his own side that did not seem to be invulnerable.....He rarely failed in gaining his cases in court. [3]

Another acquaintance said:

Mr. Lincoln had the appearance of being a slow thinker. My impression is that he was not slow as he was careful. He never liked to put forth a proposition without revolving it over in his own mind but when he was compelled to act promptly, as in debate, he was quick enough.

Someone else said of him, "He had found common sense a sure reliance and he put it into practice." [4]

2. Acceptance of self, others, nature

They "accept themselves and their own nature...."
They look upon the world as a child does, simply accepting it. They accept human nature in the same way. They have hearty appetites and enjoy sex. They have a "lack of disgust [with]...body products, body odors, and body functions." [5]

Lincoln:

His cousin said, "Abraham was a good and hearty eater—loved good eating." [6]

3. Spontanety

Their Behavior is simple and natural. They are able to cast conventionality aside if it interferes with something important. [7]

Lincoln:

A fellow attorney said:

He was the most simple, guileless, and unsophisticated man that it was possible to be. At the table, he ate what came first, without discrimination or choice; whatever bed he came to first he took without criticism or inspection; if the fire needed replenishing and no one was at hand, he made no inquiry or complaint, but hunted up an axe, took off his coat, and went vigorously at work at the wood pile.... [8]

He had no regard for trivial things, or for mere forms, manners, politeness, etiquette, official formalities, fine clothes, routine, or red tape.... [9]

A French journalist said:

His voice is far from musical; his language is not flowery; he speaks more or less like an ordinary person from the West and slang comes easily to his tongue. [10]

Frederick Douglass said:

On my approach he slowly drew his feet in from the different parts of the room into which they had strayed, and he began to rise, and continued to rise until he looked down upon me, and extended his hand and gave me a welcome. [11]

A humorist said:

He sat in the room with his boots off..., 'I like to give my feet a chance to breathe.' He had removed his coat and vest, dropped one suspender from his shoulder, taken off his necktie and collar, and thus comfortably attired, or rather unattired, he sat tilted back in one chair with his feet upon another in perfect ease....

He added:

He bubbled over with good feeling; he expressed a liking for my little work.... [12]

4. Problem centering

They generally have a mission in life, a problem outside of themselves to solve which takes much energy. [13]

Lincoln:

His purpose was to "preserve, protect and defend" the Union and to eliminate slavery. [14]

5. Need for privacy and solitude

"They positively *like* solitude and privacy...."
They do not react violently to their own personal problems.
They are calm and serene.
They can concentrate much better than ordinary people. [15]

Lincoln:

A law student said, "He would display wonderful powers of concentration." Sometimes he would grab Tad and walk onto the prairie. By the time he returned he would have the [legal] problem solved. [16]

His private secretaries reported that Lincoln was "by nature and habit so calm, so equable, so undemonstrative..." [17]

6. Autonomy

They depend on their own resources rather than looking for support from other people.

They have "a relative stability in the face of hard knocks [and] a relative serenity in the midst of circumstances that would drive other people to suicide."

They don't care about what other people think of them. [18]

Lincoln:

An attorney said:

> *As a politician and as a President he arrived at all his conclusions from his own reflections, and when his opinion was once formed he never had any doubt but what it was right.* [19]

Lincoln was able to deal with his deep grief over the death of his son Willie. At the same time he almost single-handedly raised his youngest son Tad because his wife, Mary, was in no condition to do so. He also had to decisively deal with the Civil War.

7. Freshness of appreciation

They have a "wonderful capacity to appreciate…freshly and naively the basic goods of life, with awe, pleasure, wonder and even ecstasy…." Some feel this way about nature or children or great music. [20]

Lincoln:

Julia Taft, his sons' babysitter said:

He was a "gently smiling father who played with us and told stories" when he had some time.

> *The boys would rush at him and demand a story. Tad perched precariously on the back of the big chair, Willie on one knee, Bud on the other, both leaning against him.*

Holly usually found a place on the arm of the chair, and often I would find myself swept into the group by the long arm which seemed to reach almost across the room.... [21]

Once I heard a terrible racket in another room, and opening the door...beheld the President lying on the floor, with the four boys trying to hold him down. Willie and Bud had hold of his hands, Holly and Tad sprawled over his feet and legs, while the broad grin of Mr. Lincoln's face was evidence he was enjoying himself hugely. [22]

8. Mystic experience

This is a natural experience and is a "fairly common experience for self-actualized people." [23]

Lincoln:

During the Civil War Lincoln began to feel as if there was a supreme being and that our purpose was to carry out His will. And that we could rely on Him for the wisdom and courage to do so. [24]

Earlier we discussed conversions, mostly sudden conversions. Lincoln's was gradual. When he was young he wrote an essay against Christianity which a friend wisely burned. [25] Later Herndon said Lincoln turned to God "but it was a kind of poetry...and he was never a technical Christian." [26] He believed in predestination but with it had a "profound reverence" for justice. He believed in a God who directed human affairs, who was just and merciful, *mostly just* as he said in his second inaugural: [27]

Fondly do we hope, fervently do we pray, that this mighty scourge of war may speedily pass away. Yet if God wills that it continue until all the wealth piled by the bondman's two hundred and fifty years of unrequited toil shall be sunk, and until every drop of blood drawn with the lash shall be paid with another drawn with the sword, as was said three thousand years ago, so still it must be said, "The judgements of the Lord are true and righteous altogether."

9. Gemeinschaftsgefuhl

He has *gemeinschaftsgefuhl* which describes how self-actualized people feel about human beings in general. He knows the average person has many short comings. He knows he can do many things better than they can. He knows that the truth is hidden from them. Nevertheless he "feels a basic underlying kinship with these creatures...." [28]

They are more apt to enjoy differences than to fear them accepting class, political, role and religious differences. They very much identify with humanity.

Lincoln:

A friend said:

He was remarkably tender of the feelings of others and never wantonly offended even the most despicable although he was a man of great nerve when aroused. [29]

A British journalist said:

There is about him a complete absence of pretention, and an evident desire to be courteous to everybody.... [30]

A German-American reformer said:

He received me like an old acquaintance...and we sat down together...he [told] me about the points he and Douglas had made in the debates...he asked me—a young beginner in politics—what I thought about this and that...he talked in so simple and familiar a strain, and his manner and homely phrase were so absolutely free from any semblance of self-consciousness or pretension to superiority, that I soon felt as I had known him, all my life and we had been close friends. [31]

Another man said:

When he was introduced to persons his general method was to entertain them by telling them a story, or else cross-question them along the line of their work, and soon draw from them about all the information they had. [32]

10. Interpersonal relations

They have few close friends. It seems to take up too much of their time. The people who "they love profoundly are few in number." He probably has many admirers, even worshippers but he tries to "avoid them as gracefully as possible." Their friends are much closer to self-actualization than most people. [33]

Lincoln:

Joshua Speed:

Lincoln met Joshua Speed in 1837. Speed was part owner of a general store. For 4 years they shared a bed above the store. [34]
Speed noted both the kindness of Lincoln's heart and his "nervous sensibility."
Lincoln's biographers Nicolay and Hay noted that Speed was "the only—as he was certainly the last—intimate friend that Lincoln ever had." [35]

Nicolay and Hay:

Hay during the first year of the war "accompan[ied] Lincoln almost everywhere." [36]

"Lincoln trusted his secretaries from the very beginning and they never betrayed his trust." [37] He often "shar[ed] meals with them..work[ed] with them for long hours...." He loved Hay's funny stories which were as good as his own. [38] He often turned to them for "relaxed, enjoyable conversation." [39]

William Seward:

Republican leaders wanted to remove Seward, the Secretary of State. They were jealous of his relationship with the president. Also the public felt the war was going badly and it was Seward's fault. He was called the President's de facto leader. [40] Seward's friends blocked a resolution of censure but Seward sent Lincoln a letter of resignation. The President insisted he remain in the cabinet. From that time on, Lincoln would drop by Seward's house, often unannounced, and they would talk for hours. Seward was the only person with whom Lincoln could relax. [41] Donald, his biographer, said, "Their friendship was close, warm, and even affectionate...." [42]

11. Democratic

They can be friends with anyone of "suitable character." They seem unaware of class or race or color. They can learn from anybody. They are respectful and humble when they are with others if only because they are human beings. They do display anger when confronted with evil behavior. [43]

Lincoln:

Frederick Douglass:

Frederick Douglass attended a reception on the evening of the second inauguration.

Two policemen tried to usher him out. Negroes were not allowed in the Executive Mansion. He asked a passer-by to tell the President that he was there.

President Lincoln saw him and said in a loud voice, "Here comes my friend Douglass." They shook hands and Lincoln said, "Douglass I saw you in the crowd today listening to my inaugural address. There is no man's opinion that I value more than yours: What did you think of it?" I said, "Mr. Lincoln, I cannot stop here to talk with you as there are thousands waiting to shake you by the hand;" but he said again: "What did you think of it?" I said, "Mr. Lincoln, it was a sacred effort," and then I walked off. "I'm glad you liked it," he said. [44]

Sojourner Truth, an ex-slave and evangelist said:

He showed as much kindness and consideration to the colored persons as to the whites—if there was any difference, more. [45]

Lincoln was able to express anger when it was deserved:

An officer who had been court-martialed came to see the President 3 times. On the 3rd time the man said, "Well, Mr. President, I see you are fully determined not to do me justice." Lincoln "compressed his lips... quietly arose, laid down a package of papers he held in his hand, and then suddenly seizing the...officer by the coat-collar, he marched him forcibly to the door, saying, as he ejected him into the passage: 'Sir, I give you fair warning never to show yourself in this room again. I can bear censure, but not insult!'" The man "begged for his papers. 'Begone sir,' said the President, 'your papers will be sent to you. I never wish to see your face again.'" [46]

12. They are sure about the difference between good and evil

"They have definite moral standards, they do right and do not do wrong." [47]

Lincoln:

Lincoln said, "I am naturally anti-slavery. If slavery is not wrong, nothing is wrong." [48]

13. Sense of Humor

Their sense of humor is not mean or sarcastic. It "consists in large part at poking fun at human beings in general when they are foolish, or forget their place in the universe, or try to be big when they are actually small." [49]

Lincoln:

His stories delighted himself:

A journalist said:

> *It was a joy indeed to see the effect upon him. A high-pitched laughter lightened up his otherwise melancholy countenance with thorough merriment. His body shook all over with gleeful emotion, and when he felt particularly good over his performance, he followed his habit of drawing up his knees, with his arms around them, up to his very face as I had seen him do in 1858.* [50]

Another man said:

> *His laugh was so genuine, hearty, and contagious that nobody could fail to join in.* [51]

Alexander H. Stephens, the Vice President of the Confederacy said:

His anecdotes were always exceedingly apt and pointed, and socially he always kept his company in a roar of laughter. [52]

A Congressman said:

His mirth was exuberant, it sparkled in jest, story, and anecdote....[53]

Sometimes a politician would come to see him so that he could brag about talking to the President.

His bodyguard said:

Mr. Lincoln would start in on a droll story, and when he finished the politician would be laughing so heartily he would forget all about what he was going to tell the President. Then his hand would be grasped by the President, who would at once turn to his desk, and the politician would find himself leaving the White House more than satisfied with his call, which had lasted two minutes instead of two hours as he had expected. [54]

14. Creativity

Their art is "more spontaneous, more natural, more human" than other people's.

They may apply their creativity to something more humble than writing books, composing music or producing art. [55]

Lincoln:

Lincoln's creativity was best expressed in his speeches:

The Gettysburg Address

Four Score and seven years ago our fathers brought forth on this continent, a new nation, conceived in Liberty, and dedicated to the proposition that all men are created equal.

Now we are engaged in a great civil war, testing whether that nation, or any nation so conceived and so dedicated, can long endure. We are met on a great battle-field of that war. We have come to dedicate a portion of that field, as a final resting place for those who here gave their lives that that nation might live. It is altogether fitting and proper that we should do this.

But, in a larger sense, we can not dedicate—we can not consecrate—we can not hallow—this ground. The brave men, living and dead, who struggled here, have consecrated it, far above our poor power to add or detract. The world will little note, nor long remember what we say here, but it can never forget what they did here. It is for us the living, rather, to be dedicated here to the great task remaining before us—that from these honored dead we take increased devotion to that cause for which they gave the last full measure of devotion—that we here highly resolve that these dead shall not have died in vain—that this nation, under God, shall have a new birth of freedom— and that government of the people, by the people, for the people, shall not perish from the earth.

15. Transcendence of any culture

They dress conservatively but not fashionably. They maintain a detachment from the culture in which they live. They accept unimportant matters with a "shrug of the shoulders." They "toss off" conventionality when it interferes with the truth or getting something done. They reform from within the culture rather than fighting the culture from without. [56]

Lincoln:

His step-mother said:

He "was tolerably neat and clean only - cared nothing for clothes...." [57]

A White House clerk said:

There was...what to a host of men was a provoking way of stepping over or across unessential things, with an instinctive perception of their lack of value. [58]

The Assistant Secretary of War said:

He never stepped too soon, and he never stepped too late. When the whole Northern country seemed to be clamoring for him to issue a proclamation abolishing slavery, he didn't do it. [59]

16. They are imperfect

They are good people but not perfect. They can be silly and wasteful, stubborn and irritating. They sometimes become very angry. Their great powers of concentration makes them impolite in social situations. Maslow says, "People can be found who are good, very good indeed, in fact, great." But, he says, *"There are no perfect human beings."* [60]

Lincoln:

William H. Herndon, his law partner said:

> *Lincoln never read any other way but aloud. This habit used to annoy me almost beyond the point of endurance... He paid but little attention to the fees and money matters of the firm....He was in the habit...of bringing his two boys, Willie and Thomas...down to the office to remain while his wife attended church....If they pulled all the books from the shelves, bent the points of all the pens, overturned inkstands, scattered law-papers over the floor, or threw the pencils in the spittoon, it never disturbed the serenity of their father's good-nature....*
> [61]

7

Theodore Roosevelt

He was just like a Jack coming out of the box; there wasn't anything cool about him.—Isaac Hunt, New York assemblyman

Like his hero, Abraham Lincoln, Theodore Roosevelt was also self-actualized. This is from the introduction to my book: [1]

I wrote this book because whenever I read about two brain disorders that I have, Attention Deficit Disorder and bipolar disorder, the books invariably use Theodore Roosevelt as their *poster boy*. The writers imply that if presidents have one of these disorders, it is okay for the reader to have it. For this reason I had been promising myself for years to learn about Theodore Roosevelt....

I didn't start studying him until I heard that historians ranked him as the fifth greatest president. (Now he is rated fourth, after Abraham Lincoln, F.D.R. and George Washington.) I wondered how someone with two brain disorders could be a great president.

Theodore Roosevelt had mild mood swings. "He had moods," my psychiatrist said the other day. "That doesn't mean he was bipolar," he added. [Later 2 respected writers agreed that he was mildly bipolar.] I, too, used to just have *moods*. Under extreme stress though, I ended up in the hospital and was diagnosed as bipolar.

I believe that Theodore Roosevelt, who described himself as being nervous as a youth, was aware of his tendency towards depression and anxiety. Being aware of it and wanting to be mentally healthy, he learned to control his *moods*. He became mentally healthy and this book explores how he did that. What helped his growth as a person? Carleton Putnam, who wrote *Theodore Roosevelt The Formative Years 1858-1886,* described Theodore's wonderful, even saintly parents. His father was loved by almost everyone in New York City. He founded many charities and museums. He cared for Theodore during his asthma attacks and took him to the mountains, the seashore and even to Europe to help him breathe better. He was the one who challenged Theodore to become a partner in fighting his asthma by saying "you have to make your body." This was the beginning of the realization that Theodore could do something about his problems and he became more self confident as a result. For the rest of his life, Theodore worked on building his self confidence. He constantly had to visualize himself as a hero. He was *not* naturally brave.

He was lucky too that he was brought up to love books. He was encouraged to read about any subject that interested him and later was able to read a book a day (at least).

He stumbled onto hobbies (natural history and ornithology) that forced him to focus his attention on birds and other animal life. This improved his memory and concentration.

When he was nineteen his father, who had been his best friend and confidant, died of stomach cancer. Theodore almost went crazy with grief, but the support of his family got him through this. What also helped was a trip to Maine where he met a strong, good man, Will Sewell, a hunting guide. Later he poured out his love to a girl named Alice Lee, a tall, slender blond with eyes described as "dove gray."

He married Alice, but she died after giving birth to the second Alice, Alice Roosevelt Longworth. His mother died on the same day, in the same house, Valentine's Day, 1884.

Theodore had made a promise to himself when his father died that he would become the best man possible, to honor his father's name. This promise got him through this new grief and he threw himself into his work. He was the youngest member of the New York legislature at the time.

He never made it his goal to become president. His only goal was to do the best he could with the job at hand. If he did that, he felt, the future would take care of itself.

He was the best Police Commissioner New York City ever had and he pioneered the use of forensic science in police work. Many of his guidelines are still followed. He would have earned a place in the history books just for his innovations in the New York City police department if he had not become president.

Through the intervention of some friends he was appointed Assistant Secretary of the Navy and worked to prepare the Navy for the Spanish American War. When he was thirty-nine, he resigned from that position to lead a group of volunteers to Cuba to fight in the war. He fought courageously there and later wrote an exciting book called *The Rough Riders*, which is still in print today.

After the war he became wildly popular and ran for Governor of New York and won. He did an excellent job as governor, but was "kicked upstairs" to the vice presidency by the corrupt party boss.

He felt his career was over and went on vacation as soon as he could, worried that he was facing a life of inactivity (the vice presidency not being a particularly active job.) Fate propelled Theodore Roosevelt into a job he was perfectly prepared for when President McKinley was assassinated.

He set the tone for the twentieth century Presidency. He preserved wilderness areas for future generations, mediated foreign disputes, had the Panama Canal built and arbitrated a coal strike. He loved being president, but found it troubling at times. For inspiration he read about President Lincoln who, he felt, had much more to cope with than he did.

He refused to run for a third term and instead went on a safari to Africa. He wrote magazine articles about his adventures while everyone else was taking a well deserved rest.

In 1912 he ran for president under the Progressive Party. The platform foreshadowed the New Deal of Franklin Roosevelt and was an inspiration to Franklin who idolized his Cousin Ted.

Death came suddenly on January 6, 1919, and caught Theodore sleeping. Had he not been sleeping, it was said, Roosevelt would have given Death quite a fight. He was buried in Young's Cemetery about a mile from his house. So many people trampled his grave that first year that a tall iron fence was erected around it. Even in death, Theodore Roosevelt was the most famous man in the world.

• • • • •

This is a passage from my book *The Joy of Life*. It describes a spiritual experience which Edmund Morris hinted at in his book *The Rise of Theodore Roosevelt*.

Epiphany

I think it would be wise to pause here and consider Roosevelt's spiritual orientation because it affected so much of what he did later.

In 1913 Theodore Roosevelt said William James was a "profound and lofty" thinker who was "thoroughly scientific…steeped in the teachings of material science," yet who let nothing stand in his way of his search for truth. [2] Roosevelt had a lot of respect for James and recommended the reading of *The Varieties of Religious Experience*.

The Varieties of Religious Experience gives many examples of religious or mystical experiences, explains that these experiences lead to sanctity and then step-by-step explains how sanctity expresses itself in different people. For example, the person may become self-sacrificing or find it possible to be more gentle or more tactful than was possible before. The person might also be driven to put aside material comforts to a great degree or be willing and anxious to take on unnecessary suffering.

The mystical experience makes the person see that there is a God, helps him to understand his purpose in life and usually starts him along a path towards sanctity or sainthood. This is what I believe happened to Theodore Roosevelt. Certainly he was deserving of this happening to him. He had been working on self-improvement for years. At one time he lived to please his father. Now he lived to please God, a father-like figure who was at least as kind and loving as his earthly father had been. People who have suffered and then worked, perhaps for years, on self-improvement are the type of people who have a mystical experience. It is a very common thing according to William James, who gives example after example of it in his book.

Theodore's strong feeling for his Rough Riders as expressed in his book about the war leads me to believe the life-changing experience happened then. The reason I say he must have had such an experience is because it is the only thing that can explain in my mind how he became such an extraordinary president. Without the experience he could have become a competent president, but he was far, far better than competent.

He once said that "beyond the material world lies a vast series of phenomena which all material knowledge is powerless to explain." He also, in the same lecture, quoted a philosopher who talked of a "new dimension of our environment" which "hangs over our particular physical surroundings" into which we may at any time "be plunged." [3] I think he was "plunged" into this spiritual dimension when he came to see that there is something that unites all of us, unique though we may be. He rejoiced in the uniqueness of each Rough Rider, yet saw something, their courage and spirit, uniting them.

I think he experienced an *epiphany* while training the Rough Riders, the group of men that contained half-breeds, Indians, African-Americans, marshals, Texas rangers, bear hunters, Ivy Leaguers, a Crockett, and an Adams.

This seems to be the point at which Roosevelt experienced a sudden realization that all these people of mixed ancestry, people who didn't have his pedigree (and even some who did—The Harvard contingent)—all these people suddenly seemed beautiful to him. They were wonderful and unique. Their pedigree didn't matter. He now knew for sure that the mixed blood of Americans is one of our strengths. For the rest of his life he pointed proudly to the many nationalities that converged in him—French, Scottish, Irish, English, Dutch. He was an American, too, and he wanted everybody to know that he had mixed blood. What country your ancestors came from didn't matter. You were an American now and don't let him hear you call yourself an Irish-American or a German-American. Get rid of those hyphens! You are an American.

Some people are given such a gift—a clarity of vision to see virtues that unite all people. At this point Roosevelt was focusing only on Americans, the beautiful variety of peoples that make up the American *race*.

Theodore Roosevelt proved himself an excellent leader of soldiers in this War. As a boy he had trained himself in the natural sciences. In doing that, he had trained his memory for little differences in the coloration of birds. That converted over to an ability to remember names and faces and incidents which would have been impossible for the rest of us to remember. His interest in nature led to his certainty that our natural resources should be protected. His job as Police Commissioner trained him to cooperate with the press and to deal with all sorts of people. And on, and on, and on. He was very soon to be ready to be President of the United States.

Theodore was never the same after the Spanish American War. He had always been a good man. He had always, as William James wrote, *acted as if:*

> *We can act as if there were a God; feel as if we were free; consider Nature as if she were full of special designs; lay plans as if we were to be immortal; and we find then that*

these words do make a genuine difference in our moral life. [4]

When he saw during this experience that we were all one, he saw that what one does affects the others. If he does good, it does the others good. If he does bad, it affects the others badly. He wanted to be on the side of the good, as anyone does who has had a mystical experience. He was ready to work for God, to do God's will whatever that may be. He knew he would recognize it, the will of God, when it came. God would be asking something of him soon. As William James wrote:

> *The universe…takes a turn genuinely for the worse or for the better in proportion as each one of us fulfills or evades God's demands.* [5]

Although it probably wasn't apparent to others, Theodore had changed.

He would never again make such a self-serving statement to a lobbyist as "I would like to be Assistant Secretary of the Navy" or "I wonder if they have good Civil Service Commissioners (hint)." His attitude now would be (and he said words like this more than once): "I am an instrument for the betterment of the American people. Whatever helps the people, whatever office the people need me to perform, that I will perform. I won't base my acceptance of a job on how much it pays or how important it makes me look. I am here to be used, and then thrown away when I am used up."

From now on, he would spend more time with his children. He would play with them every day and with their little cousins. He would cherish his home, Sagamore Hill. He began now to work for the benefit of the common American worker. This idea had been growing in his subconscious for a long time. As William James wrote in *The Varieties of Religious Experience,* "the process of preparation and incubation [had] proceeded far enough. It is like the proverbial last straw added to the camel's burden." His mind was thrown "into a new state of equilibrium." His mystical experience was the result of "subconscious incubation and maturing of motives deposited by the experiences of life. When ripe, the results hatch out, or burst into flower." [6]

A great man once said, "War and prison are the two ways a man can find his true self." Theodore was now in contact with his true self.

Happiness and spirituality flowed from him. Goodness radiated out from him. Almost everybody could feel it. He wanted to give his life for his country in this war and for the world in a later war, in which, sadly, he was not allowed to fight.

The happiness people found in Theodore came from:

1. The certainty that there was a God.
2. That Theodore himself was on God's side and would be useful to God.
3. "The joy," as William James said, "which may result in extreme cases from absolute self-surrender." [7]

Knowing that he was on the side of the right, Theodore had gained tremendous self-confidence.

As William James said about the results of conversion:

> *What is attained is often an altogether new level of spiritual vitality, a relatively heroic level, in which impossible things have become possible, and new energies and endurances are shown. The personality is changed the man is born anew, whether or not his psychological idiosyncrasies are what give the particular shape to his metamorphosis.* [8]

From the Afterword of The Joy of Life

Myers wrote about the voices of St. Joan of Arc:

One there has been who was born with no conspicuous strength of intellect, and in no high or powerful place, but to whom voices came from childhood onwards and brought at length a strange command—one who by mere obedience to that monitory call rose to be the savior of a great nation—one to whose lot it fell to push that obedience to its limit, and to pledge life for truth; to perish at the stake rather than disown those voices or disobey that inward law.

I speak, of course, of Joan of Arc.

Myers believed in "the possibility of an impulse from the mind's deeper strata which is so far from madness that it is wiser than our sanity itself....We need not assume that the voices which she heard were the offspring of any mind but her own, any more than we need assume that the figures in which her brave and pious impulses sometimes took external form were veritable saints."

Vita Sackville-West, St. Joan's biographer, says that according to Myers, her genius "represents the supreme and ideal sanity.... Genius...is the ready uprising of the subconscious into the realm of the conscious, and may take many forms of expression." Here she gives the example of mathematical and musical geniuses. There is no hint of any supernatural power or diseased brain in such geniuses. [9]

Theodore Roosevelt was a genius. A genius at political leadership. He himself said, "If I have anything at all resembling genius, it is the gift for leadership." [10] He had a clear vision, almost prophetic, based on what he knew of history. His closeness to nature and his ability to go into a meditative trance even as a child brought him closer to his subconscious and to a spirit world of which he admitted the existence, almost as a matter of course. Several years before he died he recommended the reading of *The Varieties of Religious Experience*, by William James, as well as other philosophical and spiritual works, so that we could try to understand the existence of a spiritual dimension as he saw it.

Your purpose in life, what you were born to do, is buried in your subconscious. That purpose is something perfectly natural for you, something suited to your personality. It in no way goes beyond or outside of what the "real you" is. In *What Are Saints?* Father Martindale says "Saints retain all the human nature that is in them, all their personal, temperamental, hereditary, educational characteristics....They retain their tendency to gentleness or to imperiosity, to sense of humour or to sense of sublimity (or to both), to timidity or to audacity, as much as anyone else does; if they are vividly intelligent men, they do not become dolts; if they are very simple men, they do not become philosophers." [11]

During your life you subconsciously prepare yourself with your hobbies, your schooling and jobs for your true purpose in life. Sometimes there seems to be no particular reason for holding a certain job. It is only later that you may recognize what that job was preparing you for. Theodore didn't know why he was drawn to politics, but once in the New York Legislature he learned to cooperate with people of all different backgrounds. His leadership ability was recognized early. He was made the leader of committees and the minority leader in the Assembly. Out West he built himself up physically, increased his self-confidence by handling dangerous situations supremely well, and led men on cattle drives. His leadership abilities were tested again at the San Juan Heights. His experience as Governor of New York and Police Commissioner of New York City tested his executive abilities.

As a child he trained his memory by becoming an amateur ornithologist and naturalist. His cousin Nicholas said, "Ornithologists in particular find it essential to watch for very small variations in color and form of birds and find it helpful to be able to detect, classify, and recall these variations without having to refer to text books." [12] His memory became so good that he was able to remember the thousands of names and faces of people he met while president. His childhood reading encouraged his photographic memory whereby he could envision a book in front of him and "read the words contained therein." This talent enabled him to come up with appropriate quotes at the appropriate times, astounding everyone.

Saint or not, he was a genius in the intuitive sense described above. He always stressed that he was a very ordinary child, trying to lead us to the conclusion that we can do it too. We can find the genius lurking in our subconscious and use it. We can discover our purpose. He used his genius for the good of the American people. This genius, for want of a better word, has a noble purpose. If he showed us anything, he taught us that it is up to us to become as healthy as we can, physically, mentally and spiritually, so that we can bring this *genius* into the light of day of our consciousness. William James said, "no outward changes of condition in life can keep the nightingale of its eternal meaning from singing in all sorts of different men's hearts....If the poor and the rich could look at each other this way...how gentle would grow their disputes! What tolerance and good humor, what willingness to live and let live, would come into the world!" [13] Morally exceptional individuals are described by William James as having souls that work and endure in obedience to some inner ideal. "Inner meaning," he said, "can be complete and valid for us also, only when the inner joy, courage, and endurance are joined with an ideal." [14]

8

In Summary

When I first started writing this book, I thought I had been cured of bipolar disorder. My research showed me that this was impossible. There is no cure for bipolar disorder. However by combining medication with psychotherapy you may be able to reduce the amount of medication you take. I found that even people with recurrent depression need to keep taking their anti-depressants to keep from having a relapse.

You who have had a severe depression and/or a manic psychosis already know you need help. This is to your advantage. Pride keeps people from seeking the help they need. Realizing that you have *reached the end of your rope*, as my grandfather used to say, pushed you to get help. First, you were pushed to get psychiatric help. As you began to feel a little bit better, even if you were an atheist, you began to pray. When the medicine began to work you began to read self-help books and continued to pray. Psychotherapy is suggested at this point, not any therapy but psychotherapy that will help change your thoughts and behavior such as Positive Psychology or Cognitive Behavioral Therapy. [1] You will begin to show others compassion because now you know how it feels to be hurting.

From this point on, a person should set aside time for meditation and prayer. I certainly didn't do this enough. I didn't know that I needed it or how healing a spiritual experience could be. Spiritual books will help especially books by M. Scott Peck, Viktor Frankl, St. Therese of Liseaux, books about saints, books by saints, books about great people and any other books that uplift your soul. Viktor Frankl's autobiography is very helpful from a spiritual standpoint and so are Thomas Merton's small spiritual books.

The cure comes when the spiritual experience does. The experience gets rid of most of your neurotic emotions. It is like your mind is wiped clean of fear, distrust, suspicion, nervousness, paranoia, self-hate and hatred of others. Finally your are normal! Better than normal—calmer, more discerning, kinder, funnier and more joyous. Finally you can face the world knowing you are as good (maybe better) than others. You are not a saint but now you can work on becoming one.

Once this happens you should explore your hobbies or interests. If a hobby isn't fun for you, drop it. Read only the kind of books you like. Do what you are drawn to do. Ask yourself if there are any other activities you might enjoy. [2] Now that you are no longer a problem to the world, ask what you can do to help the world's problems. You may have to wait patiently but something will turn up.

This is my favorite prayer and, coincidently, was Bill Wilson's favorite prayer. It helps to say it:

Prayer of St. Francis of Assisi

Lord, make me an instrument of Your peace,
Where there is hatred, let me sow love,
Where there is doubt, faith,
Where there is despair, hope,
Where there is darkness, light,
And where there is sadness, joy.
O Divine Master, grant that I may not so much need to be
consoled, as to console;
To be understood, as to understand;

To be loved, as to love;
For it is in giving that we receive—
It is in pardoning that we are pardoned;
And it is in dying that we are born to eternal life.

9

Appendix

Alcoholics Anonymous (A.A.)

The Twelve Steps

Step One: We admitted that we were powerless over alcohol—that our lives had become unmanageable.

Step Two: Came to believe that a Power greater than ourselves could restore us to sanity.

Step Three: Made a decision to turn our will and our lives over to the care of God *as we understood Him.*

Step Four: Made a searching and fearless moral inventory of ourselves.

Step Five: Admitted to God, to ourselves, and to another human being the exact nature of our wrongs.

Step Six: Were entirely ready to have God remove all these defects of character.

Step Seven: Humbly asked Him to remove our shortcomings.

Step Eight: Made a list of all persons we had harmed, and became willing to make amends to them all.

Step Nine: Made direct amends to such people wherever possible, exept when to do so would injure them or others.

Step Ten: Continued to take personal inventory and when we were wrong promptly admitted it.

Step Eleven: Sought through prayer and meditation to improve our conscious contact with God *as we understood Him,* praying only for knowledge of His will for us and the power to carry that out.

Step Twelve: Having had a spiritual awakening as the result of these steps, we tried to carry this message to alcoholics, and to practice these principles in all our affairs.

A.A. Traditions

1. Our common welfare should come first; personal recovery depends upon A.A. unity.

2. For our group purpose there is but one ultimate authority—a loving God as He may express himself in our group conscience. Our leaders are but trusted servants; they do not govern.

3. The only requirement for A.A. membership is a desire to stop drinking.

4. Each group should be autonomous except in matters affecting other groups or A.A. as a whole.

5. Each group has but one primary purpose—to carry its message to the alcoholic who still suffers.

6. An A.A. group ought never endorse, finance or lend the A.A. name to any related facility or outside enterprise, lest problems of money, property and prestige divert us from our primary purpose.

7. Every A.A. group ought to be fully self-supporting, declining outside contributions.

8. Alcoholics Anonymous should remain forever nonprofessional, but our service centers may employ special workers.

9. A.A., as such, ought never be organized; but we may create service boards or committees directly responsible to those they serve.

10. Alcoholics Anonymous has no opinion on outside issues; hence the A.A. name ought never be drawn into public controversy.

11. Our public relations policy is based on attraction rather than promotion; we need always maintain personal anonymity at the level of press, radio and films.

12. Anonymity is the spiritual foundation of all our traditions, ever reminding us to place principles before personalities.

Harry M. Tiebout, M.D.

Dr. Harry Tiebout, a psychiatrist, was involved with A.A. almost from the beginning. He said:

> *A.A. was then in its miracle phase. Everything that happened seemed strange and wonderful. Hopeless drunks were being lifted out of the gutter. Individuals who had sought every known means of help without success were*

responding to this new approach. To be close to any such
group even by proxy, was electrifying. [1]

Tiebout had two very difficult patients, both narcissistic and
both alcoholics. Once exposed to A.A., they totally changed their
outlook. Before, they had resisted him at every turn. Now he
could make some headway with them. He was extremely excited.
Ever since then he endorsed A.A. as a way to approach psychiatric
problems. [2]

Dr. Harry M. Tiebout says in *Alcoholics Anonymous Comes of*
Age, A Brief History of A.A. that A.A. is "a therapeutic program
which includes a definite religious element." He gives an example of a difficult patient whose character changed suddenly after
joining A.A. He says before A.A. she had a "narcissistic egocentric
core."

For narcissism to be broken down, the alcoholic *must* accept
the presence of a higher power. Once he does that, he can give
up alcohol. No one knows how this happens. Some say he "got
religion." Some say he hypnotized himself.

Little by little, Dr. Tiebout's patient changed. No longer was
she so defensive, aggressive and suspicious. She now had a look
of peace about her. The lines in her face had softened and she
looked kinder.

Once the alcoholic changes from asking for help to asking how
they can help, the spiritual change has occurred. But the danger is
she may think that a miracle has occurred and she doesn't need to
do the 12 Step work anymore. She is wrong about this. She needs
to keep repeating the 12 Steps and when she gets to Step 12, she
needs to help the other person. The alcoholic also needs to keep
attending meetings in order to belong to something bigger than
herself.

A.A. believes that the alcoholic has to become totally humble
before the religious experience can happen. The person needs to
let go of their egocentricity enough to rely on outside help. Once

they lose their negative feelings they find themselves in a new "mental state" of calmness, peacefulness, love and friendliness.

Letting go of their narcissism allows them to become much more mature and objective. Most AA's become mature by a slow process of spiritual growth and not by a sudden conversion. But once they reach maturity, they are healed of their alcoholism.

A.A. uses "a religious or spiritual force to attack the fundamental narcissism of the alcoholic." The hostility of the alcoholic is overthrown and in its' place comes peace and harmony. Narcissism is assaulted and is neutralized. Once this has happened, the alcoholic is ready to work on understanding themselves. [3]

Narcissistic Personality Disorder (NPD)

Dr. Tiehout felt that all alcoholics have what is now known as Narcissistic Personality Disorder (NPD). This can't be true. Only 1% of the world's population has NPD. At least 8% (and probably many more) are alcoholics. The person with NPD is unlikely to admit they are alcoholic and go to an A.A. meeting. We all have some narcissism that we try to chip away at and alcoholics do have neuroses but NPD is a very severe disorder.

The symptoms of NPD (also called severe egocentrism) are:

- sense of entitlement—feels entitled to things or to special treatment
- grandiose behavior
- exploits others
- strong need for admiration
- excessively preoccupied with prestige, vanity, themselves, money or power
- lack of empathy
- fantasies of great success, intelligence, beauty
- believe they are special

- envious of others
- arrogant
- controlling
- unable to tolerate criticism
- blaming others for their problems
- think they are better than others

People who don't go along with their grandiosity are seen as worthless. The person with the disorder has delusions about the worth of their accomplishments. Other people are there only to give them admiration.

In reality they believe that they are so flawed that if others really knew them, they would reject them. NPD is a defense against their feelings of being inferior and unloved.

Possible causes of NPD

- Born overly sensitive
- Excessively admired during childhood, admiration un-balanced by realism
- Excessive praise or excessive criticism in childhood
- Overindulged by parents, relatives and peers
- Overpraised for looks or abilities
- Severe emotional abuse in childhood
- Unreliable caregiving from parents
- Used by parents to raise their own self-esteem

People with NPD have a hard time asking for help. They are too proud to admit they need it. They are defiant, sure of themselves, have no guilt and no humility. They are unable to see themselves as they really are. They need to dominate others whom they see only as an extension of themselves. I just don't think many members of A.A. have NPD. [4]

Self-actualized people

Self-actualized people worth studying

Abraham Maslow in his book *Motivation and Personality* made educated guesses as to which historical figures were self-actualized. He divided them into 3 categories: fairly sure, highly probable, and possible. On page 152 he lists them. (I have added a few of my own):

Fairly sure

- Lincoln in his last years - greatest U.S. president
- Thomas Jefferson - writer of the Declaration of Independence
- St. Therese of Lisieux - saint; wrote *Story of a Soul*
- Pope John Paul II - helped end Communist rule
- Mother Teresa - won 1979 Nobel Peace Prize

Highly probable

- Eleanor Roosevelt - most admired first lady
- Albert Einstein - won 1921 Nobel Prize in Physics
- Richard P. Feynman - won 1965 Nobel Prize in Physics
- Jane Addams - first woman to receive the Nobel Peace Prize
- William James - philosopher and psychologist
- Albert Schweitzer - 1952 Nobel Peace Prize
- Aldous Huxley - writer
- Spinoza - philosopher
- Theodore Roosevelt - first U.S. president to win the Nobel Peace Prize

Possible

- Franklin D. Roosevelt - U.S. president - only one to serve 3 terms and part of a 4th
- Adlai Stevenson - politician
- Anne Morrow Lindbergh - poet and writer
- Charles A. Lindbergh - pilot, explorer, writer
- Benjamin Franklin - Founding Father of the U.S.
- G.W. Carver - born into slavery; scientist
- Eugene V. Debs - American union leader
- Thomas Eakins - realistic painter
- Fritz Kreisler - Austrian-born violinist and composer
- Goethe - German writer, artist, politician
- Pablo Casals - Spanish cellist and conductor
- Martin Buber - Austrian-born Israeli Jewish philosopher
- Danilo Dolci - Italian social activist, educator, poet
- Arthur E. Morgan - first chairman of Tennessee Valley Authority
- John Keats - poet
- David Hilbert - German mathematician
- Arthur Waley - English orientalist and sinologist
- D.T. Suzuki - Japanese author who wrote books on Buddhism, Zen and Shin
- Sholom Aleichem - Yiddish author and playwright
- Robert Browning - poet and playwright
- Ralph Waldo Emerson - American essayist, lecturer and poet
- Frederick Douglass - American social reformer, orator, writer and statesman
- Joseph Schumpeter - Austrian-American economist and political scientist
- Bob Benchley - American humorist and film actor
- Ida Tarbell - teacher, author, journalist, *muckraker*
- Harriet Tubman - abolitionist, humanitarian, and Union spy

- George Washington - first president of the U.S.
- Karl Muenzinger - teacher and psychologist
- Joseph Haydn - Austrian composer
- Camille Pissarro - Danish-French impressionist
- Edward Bibring - Jewish doctor and psychoanalyst
- George William Russell (A.E.) - poet and educator
- Pierre Renoir - French artist
- Hanry Wadsworth Longfellow - American poet and educator
- Peter Kropotkin - Russian zoologist, philosopher, scientist, economic activist, writer
- John Atgeld - Governor of Illinois, leader of the Progressive movement
- Thomas More - English saint, lawyer, philosopher
- Edward Bellamy - American author and socialist
- John Muir - Scottish-American naturalist, author, early conservationist
- Walt Whitman [5] - American poet, essayist, journalist

Bibliography

Alcoholics Anonymous Comes of Age A Brief History of A.A., Alcoholics Anonymous World Services, Inc., New York: 1957, 1985

Alcoholics Anonymous, The Story of How Many Thousands of Men and Women Have Recovered from Alcoholism, third edition, New York: Alcoholics Anonymous World Services, Inc., 1976

'Pass It On' The Story of Bill Wilson and how the A.A. message reached the world, Alcoholics Anonymous World Services, Inc., New York, N.Y.: 1984

William Barton, *The Soul of Abraham Lincoln,* Chicago: University of Illinois Press, 2005

A Benedictine Nun of Stanbrook Abbey, *Anne—The Life of Venerable Anne de Guigne 1911-1922,* Rockford, Illinois 61165: Tan books and Publishers, Inc.

David D. Burns, M.D., *Feeling Good, The New Mood Therapy,* New York: Harper Collins Publishers, 1980

David Herbert Donald, *"We Are Lincoln Men"—Abraham Lincoln and His Friends,* New York: Simon & Schuster, 2003

The Papers of Dwight David Eisenhower, Nato and the Campaign of 1952: XIII, Baltimore, Md.: The Johns Hopkins University Press, 1989

Jan Fawcet, M.D., Bernard Golden, Ph.D., and Nancy Rosenfeld, *New Hope for People With Bipolar Disorder,* New York: Random House, Inc., 2000

Viktor E. Frankl,*Man's Search for Meaning,* New York: Washington Square Press, 1963

Frederick K. Goodwin, MD, Kay Redfield Jamison, Ph.D., *Manic-Depressive Illness, Bipolar Disorders and Recurrent Depression,* Oxford New York: Oxford University Press, 2007

Capt. Al Haynes, *The Crash of United Flight 232:* 1991

Edited by Harold Holzer, *Lincoln As I Knew Him, Gossip, Tributes, And Revelations From His Best Friends And Worst Enemies,* Chapel Hill, Algonquin books, 1999

Robert D. Isett, Ph.D., *Think Right, Feel Right, The Building Block Guide For Happiness and Emotional Well-Being,* amazon. com, 2009

William James,*The Varieties of Religious Experience—A Study in Human Nature,* New York: The Modern Library, 1999

William James, *Writings 1878-1899,* New York: Viking Press, 1992

Kay Redfield Jamison, *An Unquiet Mind,* New York: Vintage books A division of Random House, Inc., 1995

Kay Redfield Jamison, *Touched With Fire, Manic-Depressive Illness and the Artistic Temperament*, New York, NY: 1993

Broadcast by C.C. Martindale, S.J., *What Are Saints? Fifteen Chapters in Sanctity*, New York, Sheed & Ward, 1937

Abraham H. Maslow, *Motivation and Personality*, second edition, New York: Harper and Row, Publishers, 1970

William Lee Miller, *Lincoln's Virtues - An Ethical Biography*, New York: Vintage books, 2002

Theodore Roosevelt, *Selected Works of Theodore Roosevelt, Vol. VI*, "History as Literature, IX. The Search for Truth in a Reverent Spirit," 1913, New York: New Bartleby Library, 1998. On LIne Ed: Feb 1998, Bartleby.com, Steven H. van Leeuwen. Originally New York: Charles Scribner's Sons, 1913

Nicholas Roosevelt, *Theodore Roosevelt, The Man as I Knew Him*, New York: Dodd, Mead & Company, 1967

Mary Beth Smith, *The Joy of Life, A Biography of Theodore Roosevelt*, amazon.com, 2013

Vita Sackville-West, *St. Joan of Arc*, New York: Image books, Doubleday, 1991

Edward Wagenknecht, *The Seven Worlds of Theodore Roosevelt*, New York: Longmans, Green & Co., 1958

Dr. Claire Weekes, M.B.D.Sc., M.R.A.C.P., *Hope and Help for Your Nerves*, New York: Hawthorne books, Inc.—Publishers, 1969

http://www.addictiontribe.com/health/art

Behavioral Modification Cured My Bipolar Disease http://voices.yahoo.com/behavioral-modification-cured-bipolar-disease-2649273.html

http://bipolar.about.com/od/relateddisorders/a/postpartum-psych.html

http://dune.wika.com/wiky/Litany_Against_Fear

http://www.melanies battle.org/about.html

Postpartum psychosis http://www.npr_org/programs/morning/features/2002/feb/postpartum/020218.postpartum.html

http://en.wikipedia.org/wiki/Bill W.

http://en.wikipedia.org/wiki/Narcissistic_personality_disorder

Author Bio

Mary Beth Smith graduated from the College of Notre Dame of Maryland. She lives in Florida with her husband, novelist G. Ernest Smith, dog Bailey and 3 cats—Topper, Corky and Chloe. She enjoys sailing, reading and writing.

Comments concerning this book would be appreciated. Email mary_smith1949@yahoo.com

Endnotes

1
Manic-Depressive Illnesses and Recurrent Depression

[1] Kay Redfield Jamison, *Touched With Fire, Manic-Depressive Illness and the Artistic Temperament,* New York, NY: 1993, 13

[2] Frederick K. Goodwin, MD, Kay Redfield Jamison, Ph.D., *Manic-Depressive Illness, Bipolar Disorders and Recurrent Depression,* Oxford New York: Oxford University Press, 2007, 95 hereafter Goodwin Text

[3] Fire, 13

[4] Fire, 27

[5] Fire, 41

[6] Jan Fawcet, M.D., Bernard Golden, Ph.D., and Nancy Rosenfeld, *New Hope for People With Bipolar Disorder,* New York: Random House, Inc., 2000, 39 hereafter referred to as New Hope.

[7] Fire, 18-21

[8] Fire, 23

[9] Goodwin text, 98

[10] Fire, 14

[11] New Hope, 41

[12] New Hope, 43

[13] Goodwin Text, 96

[14] Goodwin Text, 99

[15] New Hope, 45

[16] http://bipolar.about.com/od/relateddisorders/a/postpartum-psych.html

[17] Goodwin text, 107

[18] *Postpartum psychosis* http://www.npr_org/programs/morning/features/2002/feb/postpartum/020218.postpartum.html

[19] http://www.melanies battle.org/about.html

[20] New Hope, 49-50

[21] Goodwin text, 135-138

[22] Fire, 155

[23] New Hope, 54

[24] New Hope, 60

[25] Fire, 252

[26] Fire, 193

[27] Goodwin text, 393

[28] Fire, 81-84

[29] Goodwin text, 381

[30] Goodwin text 386-388

[31] Goodwin text, 277-281

[32] Goodwin text, 281

[33] Fire, 87-89

[34] Goodwin text, 813-814

[35] Goodwin text, 844 notes 11 and 12

[36] http://www.addictiontribe.com/health/art

[37] Unquiet Mind, 102

[38] Goodwin text, 793 and 809

[39] New Hope, 82

2
My Story

[1] http://dune.wika.com/wiky/Litany_Against_Fear

3
Cognitive Therapy

[1] Dr. Claire Weekes, M.B.D.Sc., M.R.A.C.P., *Hope and Help for Your Nerves*, New York: Hawthorne books, Inc.—Publishers, 1969, 78, hereafter Weekes.

[2] Robert D. Isett, *Think Right, Feel Right, The Building Block Guide For Happiness and Emotional Well-Being*, Ph.D., ix-9, hereafter Isett

[3] David D. Burns, M.D., *Feeling Good, The New Mood Therapy*, New York: Harper Collins Publishers, 1980, xi-xii, hereafter Burns.

[4] Burns, xix-xxiii

[5] Burns, 461-462

[6] Fire, 247

[7] Burns, 476.

[8] Burns, 462-468

[9] Islett, 19

[10] Burns, 67-77

[11] Islett, 161

[12] Burns, 417-419

[13] Islett, 89-91

[14] Burns, 347

¹⁵ Burns, 353-359

¹⁶ Weekes, 112

¹⁷ Weekes, 115

¹⁸ Burns, 81-125

¹⁹ Weekes, 16

²⁰ Weekes, 39-40

²¹ Weekes, 52-55

²² Burns, 131-147

²³ Burns, 317-321

²⁴ Burns, 222-223

²⁵ Weekes, 98

4
Alcoholics Anonymous

¹ *Behavioral Modification Cured My Bipolar Disease* http://voices.yahoo.com/behavioral-modification-cured-bipolar-disease-2649273.html

² Bill W.—Wikipedia, the free encyclopedia

³ *'Pass It On' The Story of Bill Wilson and how the A.A. message reached the world*, Alcoholics Anonymous World Services, Inc., New York, N.Y.: 1984, 86-102, hereafter biobill.

[4] biobill, 110-111

[5] *Alcoholics Anonymous Comes of Age A Brief History of A.A.,* Alcoholics Anonymous World Services, Inc. New York: 1957, 1985, 45-59, hereafter brief hist.

[6] biobill, 110-119

[7] biobill, 120-125

[8] biobill 132-133

[9] brief hist, 13

[10] brief hist, 67

[11] brief hist 67-68

[12] biobill, p. 149

[13] biobill, 151

[14] brief hist, 39

[15] brief hist, 74-75

[16] brief hist 302-305

[17] biobill, 381-382

[18] brief hist, 265

[19] biobill, 252

[20] biobill, 196-198

[21] brief hist, 162-163

[22] brief hist, 167

[23] brief hist, 81

[24] biobill, 293-303

[25] biobill, 237

[26] biobill 306-319

[27] brief hist 102-103

[28] brief hist, 191

[29] biobill, 246-248

[30] biobill, 233

[31] biobill, 222

[32] brief hist, 204

[33] biobill, 393

[34] brief hist, 123

[35] brief hist, 316

5
Conversion
[1] Capt. Al Haynes, *The Crash of United Flight 232*: 1991

[2] *The Papers of Dwight David Eisenhower, Nato and the Campaign of 1952: XIII,* Baltimore, Md.: The Johns Hopkins University Press, 1989, 859

[3] *Alcoholics Anonymous, The Story of How Many Thousands of Men and Women Have Recovered from Alcoholism,* third edition, New York: Alcoholics Anonymous World Services, Inc., 1976, 14, hereafter AA.

[4] *The Varieties of Religious Experience—A Study in Human Nature,* William James, New York: The Modern Library, 1999, 252 hereafter Varieties

[5] Varieties, 261

[6] Varieties, 246

[7] Varieties, 268

[8] Varieties, 281

[9] Varieties, 223

[10] Varieties, 243

[11] Varieties, 284

[12] Beers, 45

[13] A Benedictine Nun of Stanbrook Abbey, *Anne—The Life of Venerable Anne de Guigne 1911-1922,* Rockford, Illinois 61165: Tan books and Publishers, Inc.

[14] Viktor E. Frankl, *Man's Search for Meaning,* New York: Washington Square Press, 1963, 207-208

[15] AA, 14

[16] *What Are Saints? Fifteen Chapters in Sanctity*, Broadcast by C.C. Martindale, S.J., New York, Sheed & Ward, 1937 hereafter Martindale

[17] Martindale, 100

[18] Martindale, 118-119

[19] Martindale, 145-147

6
Mental Health

[1] Abraham H. Maslow, *Motivation and Personality*, second edition, New York: Harper and Row, Publishers, 1970, 150, hereafter Maslow.

[2] Maslow, 153

[3] Edited by Harold Holzer,*Lincoln As I Knew Him, Gossip, Tributes, And Revelations From His Best Friends And Worst Enemies*, Chapel Hill, Algonquin books, 1999, 42, hereafter Holzer.

[4] Holzer, 38

[5] Maslow, 155-156

[6] Holzer, 23

[7] Maslow, 157-158

[8] Holzer, 65

[9] Holzer, 65

[10] Holzer, 117

[11] Holzer, 203

[12] Holzer, 97-101

[13] Maslow, 159

[14] William Barton, *The Soul of Abraham Lincoln,* Chicago: University of Illinois Press, 2005, 292, hereafter Barton.

[15] Maslow, 160

[16] Holzer, 73

[17] Holzer, 214

[18] Maslow, 162

[19] Holzer, 81

[20] Maslow, 163

[21] Holzer, 224

[22] Holzer, 225

[23] Maslow, 164

[24] Barton, 231

[25] Barton, 229

[26] Barton, 230

[27] Barton, 231

[28] Maslow, 165-166

[29] Holzer, 70

[30] Holzer, 120, 121

[31] Holzer, 55-56

[32] Holzer, 77

[33] Maslow, 166

[34] David Herbert Donald, *"We Are Lincoln Men"—Abraham Lincoln and His Friends,* New York: Simon & Schuster, 2003, 32, hereafter Donald.

[35] Donald, 34-35

[36] Donald, 178

[37] Donald, 189

[38] Donald, 194

[39] Donald, 178

[40] Donald, 165-166

[41] Donald, 168-169

[42] Donald, 170

[43] Maslow, 167-168

[44] Holzer, 207-208

[45] Holzer, 199

[46] Holzer, 195

[47] Maslow, 168

[48] William Lee Miller, *Lincoln's Virtues - An Ethical Biography*, New York: Vintage books, 2002, 275

[49] Maslow 169-170

[50] Holzer, 94

[51] Holzer, 56

[52] Holzer, 140

[53] Holzer, 48

[54] Holzer, 243-244

[55] Maslow, 171

[56] Maslow, 171-172

[57] Holzer, 16-17

[58] Holzer, 230

[59] Holzer, 147

[60] Maslow 174-176

[61] Holzer, 68-69

7
Theodore Roosevelt

[1] *The Joy of Life, A Biography of Theodore Roosevelt,* Mary Beth Smith, amazon.com, 2013

[2] Theodore Roosevelt, *Selected Works of Theodore Roosevelt, Vol. VI,* "History as Literature, IX. The Search for Truth in a Reverent Spirit," 1913, New York: New Bartleby Library, 1998. On LIne Ed: Feb 1998, Bartleby.com, Steven H. van Leeuwen. Originally New York: Charles Scribner's Sons, 1913. Hereafter hist.

[3] hist, paragraph 14

[4] Varieties, 55

[5] Varieties, 507

[6] Varieties, 226

[7] Varieities, 72

[8] Varieties, 236

[9] Vita Sackville-West, *St. Joan of Arc,* New York: Image books, Doubleday, 1991, 330-336

[10] Edward Wagenknecht, *The Seven Worlds of Theodore Roosevelt,* New York: Longmans, Green & Co., 1958, 152

[11] Martindale, 152-153

[12] Nicholas Roosevelt, *Theodore Roosevelt, The Man as I Knew Him,* New York: Dodd, Mead & Company, 1967, 60

[13] William James, *Writings 1878-1899,* New York: Viking Press, 1992, 879-880, hereafter James.

[14] James, 873-875

8
In Summary

[1] Islett, 169

[2] Islett, 169

9
Appendix

[1] brief hist, 246

[2] brief hist, 3

[3] brief hist, 309-319

[4] http://en.wikipedia.org/wiki/Narcissistic_personality_disorder

[5] Maslow, 152